T0288275

CONCISE
LINCOLN
LIBRARY

—

EDITED BY RICHARD W. ETULAIN
AND SYLVIA FRANK RODRIGUE

STANLEY HARROLD

Lincoln and the Abolitionists

Southern Illinois University Press
Carbondale

Southern Illinois University Press
www.siupress.com

21 20 19 18   4 3 2 1

The Concise Lincoln Library has been made possible
in part through a generous donation by the Leland
E. and LaRita R. Boren Trust.

Volumes in this series have been published with
support from the Abraham Lincoln Bicentennial
Foundation, dedicated to perpetuating and expanding Lincoln's vision for America and completing
America's unfinished work.

Jacket illustration adapted from a painting by
Wendy Allen

Library of Congress Cataloging-in-Publication Data
Names: Harrold, Stanley.
Title: Lincoln and the abolitionists / Stanley
Harrold.
Description: Carbondale : Southern Illinois Univer-
sity Press, 2018. | Series: Concise Lincoln library
| Includes bibliographical references and index.
Identifiers: LCCN 2017026601 | ISBN
9780809336418 (cloth : alk. paper) | ISBN
9780809336425 (e-book)
Subjects: LCSH: Lincoln, Abraham, 1809–1865—
Views on slavery. | Abolitionists—United States—
History—19th century. | Antislavery movements—
United States—History—19th century.
Classification: LCC E457.2 .H35 2018
| DDC 973.7092—dc23
LC record available at https://lccn.loc
.gov/2017026601

Printed on recycled paper. ♻

This paper meets the requirements of ANSI/NISO
Z39.48-1992 (Permanence of Paper) ∞

For Doug Egerton and Jack Kaufman-McKivigan

CONTENTS

Gallery of illustrations beginning on page 41

LINCOLN AND THE ABOLITIONISTS

INTRODUCTION

On April 14, 1876, black and white Americans gathered in Washington, D.C., to dedicate the Freedmen's Monument. The monument consists of a sculpture that depicts Abraham Lincoln standing benignly over a chained, kneeling black man who represents American slaves freed during the Civil War. Well before the unveiling of the monument, which occurred on the eleventh anniversary of Lincoln's assassination, he had become known as the "Great Emancipator." The monument reflects the belief that he had achieved what abolitionists, slavery's most radical opponents, had for decades advocated: freedom and equal rights for all African Americans.

As Frederick Douglass, the country's leading black abolitionist and a powerful force within the abolition movement, delivered the dedication ceremony's keynote address, he complicated this assumption. According to Douglass, Lincoln had been "preeminently the white man's President, entirely devoted to the welfare of white men." During the early years of the Civil War, Lincoln, in Douglass's recollection, had been "willing . . . to deny, postpone, and sacrifice the rights of humanity in the colored people to promote the welfare of the white people of this country." From a "genuine abolition" perspective, "Lincoln seemed tardy, cold, dull, and indifferent."[1]

Lincoln, as Douglass observed, "shared the prejudices common to his countrymen towards the colored race." Prior to the Civil War abolitionists in the North had demanded the immediate abolition of slavery throughout the country. Lincoln had at best opposed "the extension of slavery" from the southern states into America's western territories. During the war's first two years he sought chiefly to preserve the Union on behalf of the interests of white northerners, even as abolitionists urged him to act against slavery in the southern states and the national domain. Yet, as Douglass and many other abolitionists came to realize, had Lincoln "put the abolition of slavery before the salvation of the Union, he would have driven from him a powerful class of the American people and rendered resistance to the rebellion impossible."[2] This in turn would have made the abolitionist goal of universal emancipation and equal rights impossible as well.

Douglass's ambivalent view of Lincoln was not new, and Lincoln had an ambivalent view of abolitionists as well. This book therefore describes a long, complex, and ultimately direct relationship between politician Lincoln and a group of radical reformers determined to control U.S. policy regarding slavery. The story is set in a nation increasingly divided over the slavery issue. The division existed not only between the North and South but within the North where attitudes toward slavery and black rights ranged widely. The *abolitionists* regarded slavery to be a sin and crime that must quickly end. Many other northerners sympathized with white southerners, held staunchly racist views of African Americans, and opposed granting them equal rights in the United States. And there were those, such as Lincoln, who merely disliked slavery. They were *antislavery* in that they did not believe slavery was a beneficial labor system, did not want slavery to expand, and worried about slaveholder domination of the U.S. government. But they sought compromise with the white South, opposed abolitionist radicalism, and doubted that free black people could have a positive role in America.

From the time Lincoln first ran for elective office in 1832, he remained a politician who sought to represent his constituents' views and desires on a wide range of issues that went beyond slavery in the South. For two decades he identified with the Whig Party. This political organization for much of its existence represented upwardly mobile northerners, national government encouragement of industry, moderate white southerners concentrated in the Border South, *and* evangelically oriented northerners who opposed slavery for religious reasons. For much of his life Lincoln idealized Whig leader Henry Clay, a Kentucky slaveholder who mildly opposed slavery and sought sectional reconciliation. Born in Kentucky and competing for political office in Illinois against Democratic Party candidates who were much more proslavery and antiblack than he, Lincoln followed Clay's example. Even as the slavery expansion issue and attempts to enforce the Fugitive Slave Law of 1850 destroyed the Whig Party, Lincoln maintained a moderate position. Yet remote as he initially stood physically and intellectually from abolitionists, they fundamentally influenced his evolving political orientation. In the end, he influenced them as well.

DIFFERENT WORLDS

During the first three decades of his life, Abraham Lincoln had little or no direct contact with abolitionists. He grew up in the frontier conditions of Kentucky and Indiana, amid poverty, family tragedy, and lack of access to formal education. His priorities included educating himself, finding work more rewarding than physical labor, and beginning a political career. The last of these required that he stay within a locally acceptable range of opinion regarding public policy, slavery, and black rights. The abolition movement's center lay far to the east in an area stretching from eastern Pennsylvania northward into New England. Yet, by the time Lincoln reached adulthood, abolitionists had helped shape conditions in the United States, including Illinois, to which his family moved in 1830, when he was twenty-one. As a politician, he had to deal with issues abolitionists helped raise even as their movement changed its character and faced political and physical challenges.

At the time of Lincoln's birth on February 12, 1809, at a primitive farm on the northwestern edge of the slave-labor state of Kentucky, an organized American movement to abolish slavery had existed for over three decades. The Pennsylvania Abolition Society (PAS) best represented the movement, which concentrated on ending slavery in the northeastern states. The society had grown out of a religiously based effort dominated by Quakers stretching back into the late seventeenth century. It came into existence as a result of the American Revolution and added the Declaration of Independence's equal rights principles to Quaker pacifism and commitment to love one's neighbor as the abolition movement's guiding principles. The movement soon spread into New England as black and white abolitionists petitioned state legislatures and sued for emancipation. Between 1780 in Pennsylvania and 1804 in New Jersey, such efforts contributed to legislative action or court rulings ending slavery either immediately or gradually throughout the Northeast. Loosely organized in the American Convention for Promoting the Abolition of Slavery (hereafter American Convention), abolitionists also contributed to a wave of manumissions in Delaware, Maryland, and Virginia.[1]

During the late eighteenth century many Americans, north and south of the Mason-Dixon Line, expected emancipation to spread throughout the South and end slavery. That hope faded as a result of Eli Whitney's invention of the cotton gin in 1793. By speeding the separation of cotton seeds from cotton fiber, Whitney's simple machine made cotton America's most profitable product. This in turn increased demand for slave labor and encouraged slavery's spread westward across the South to beyond the Mississippi River. By the late 1820s masters and slaves had reached the Mexican province of Texas. Economic interest, a white southern imperative to control African Americans, and diverging moralities set the South on a path different from the North's.

So did the abolitionist encouragement of emancipation in the northeastern states. The decline and disappearance of slavery in these states contributed to the growth of a northern economy based on wage labor. That economy in turn encouraged northern politicians to challenge slaveholding interests. Northeastern emancipation also allowed for limited freedom among African Americans in that region. But, for Lincoln and others raised on America's northwestern frontier during the 1810s and 1820s, abolitionist victories in the Northeast seemed far away, not especially relevant, and at times disturbing. The increasingly commercial Northeast nurtured a physical and intellectual environment quite different from the rural conditions existing in Kentucky and southern Indiana during Lincoln's early years. Into the Civil War years he owed the bulk of his views concerning slavery *not* to northern abolitionists but to the thought, policies, and actions of slaveholders Thomas Jefferson of Virginia and Henry Clay of Kentucky. Jefferson wrote the Declaration of Independence and served as ambassador to France during the American Revolution. He was also George Washington's secretary of state and U.S. president. Clay served as Speaker of the House, John Quincy Adams's secretary of state, and U.S. senator. Each of these major politicians professed to oppose slavery, continued to own slaves, endorsed only very gradual emancipation schemes, rejected black equality, and denounced abolitionists.[2]

Lincoln's family background, like his geographical location, inclined him to accept Jefferson's and Clay's views on slavery. His parents, Thomas and Nancy Lincoln, like other poor farmers in early nineteenth-century Kentucky, did not own slaves. They belonged to a local Baptist church that excluded slaveholders. But they were not abolitionists or sympathetic to African Americans. Rather Thomas Lincoln, as did many white men in the region, believed enslaved black labor demeaned white labor, made white labor less valuable and less well rewarded. This perspective, not Christian morality or the Declaration of Independence, contributed to Thomas's decision in 1816 to move his family from Hardin County, Kentucky, to Perry County, Indiana, located just north of the Ohio River. Insecure land titles in Kentucky provided an even more compelling motive. Proslavery influences remained strong in Indiana and Illinois, where the Lincolns moved to in 1830. And unlike a few religiously motivated white southern abolitionists, such as John Rankin and Levi Coffin, who moved north during these years to southern Ohio and southern Indiana respectively, the Lincolns did not aid fugitive slaves.[3]

* * *

In 1864, a year before he died, Abraham Lincoln claimed that as long as he could remember he had been "naturally anti-slavery." He wrote, "If slavery is not wrong, nothing is wrong."[4] But being "anti-slavery" was not the same thing as being an abolitionist. And there is no evidence that Lincoln, during his formative years, regarded black bondage as a major issue or that he (in contrast to white abolitionists) interacted with slaves or free African Americans. He probably did not meet an abolitionist prior to the 1840s. Nevertheless abolitionists influenced the region and state where he began his political career.

Beginning in February 1819, when Lincoln turned ten, opposition to admitting Missouri Territory (located directly to the west of Illinois) to the Union as a slave-labor state caused an intersectional crisis. In language that influenced northern politicians, abolitionist Theodore Dwight, acting on behalf of the New York Manumission Society and the American Convention, petitioned Congress to adopt "such provisions, as will exclude slavery from the limits of such territorial governments as may hereafter be established in our country." Dwight also called on Congress to "prevent any such future territory from being erected into a state, unless slavery shall be prohibited by the constitution thereof." Such abolitionist, and abolitionist-inspired, opposition to the admission of Missouri to the Union as a slave-labor state pressured Congress, under Henry Clay's guidance, to pass the Missouri Compromise in 1820. This agreement, supported by northerners and southerners, admitted Missouri with slavery. But it also banned slavery from the rest of the Louisiana Purchase north of the 36°30′ line of latitude. And it admitted Maine as a free-labor state to balance Missouri. Into the 1850s this compromise shaped Lincoln's and most other white northerners' outlooks toward slavery expansion.[5]

Another abolitionist effort had even more significance in establishing the political environment in which Lincoln came to maturity and subsequently thought and acted. In 1823 and 1824 Illinois governor Edward Coles, a former Virginian who had freed his slaves and brought them to Illinois in 1819, confronted a movement designed to legalize slavery in the state. To prevent such legalization, local abolitionists, including Baptists, Quakers, journalists, and politicians, in March 1823 organized societies dedicated to "the prevention of slavery in the State of Illinois." To assist them, PAS leader Roberts Vaux of Philadelphia (who recognized western distaste for northeastern abolitionists) discreetly sent six thousand antislavery pamphlets to Coles for "gratuitous distribution." When Illinois voters rejected holding a state constitutional convention that could have legalized slavery, Coles secured legislation providing for "speedy . . . abolition" and "severe penalties" for kidnapping free African Americans into slavery.[6] Therefore abolitionists had a role in creating the economic and political culture of Lincoln's adopted state. By contributing to Illinois' maintaining its status as a free-labor state, they also affected the nature of the sectional conflict that, over the years, determined the course of Lincoln's political career.

Yet support for abolitionism "dramatically waned" in Illinois after 1823. As in western Kentucky, much of the opposition to slavery among Illinois' white residents had rested on antiblack prejudice rather than abolitionist concern for morality and black rights. Many in Illinois, beyond those such as the Lincolns who came from the Border South, believed slavery negatively affected "poor white" living conditions. They charged that slavery forced white men to work beside black men and compete with black men for jobs. They had little sympathy for free African Americans who lived in Illinois. Even as the state preserved its free-labor status, its legislature during the 1820s and 1830s joined Ohio's and Indiana's in restricting black settlement. These states also barred black men from voting, serving in the militia, and testifying in court against white people. In 1840 the Will County, Illinois, Anti-Slavery Society published a pamphlet describing Illinois' version of these oppressive laws. In response America's best-known abolitionist, William Lloyd Garrison, exclaimed in his *Liberator* newspaper, "O most detestable and bloody State! Thy offense is rank, 'and smells to heaven.'"[7]

In contrast Abraham Lincoln, who shared the great majority of white Illinoisans' racial views, did not denounce the laws. Although he may have been "naturally anti-slavery," as a young adult he concentrated on advancing himself intellectually, economically, and politically. In 1831 at age twenty-two, he moved from his father's central Illinois cabin to New Salem, located in the western part of the state. There he continued his self-education and during March 1832 entered politics in an unsuccessful campaign for a seat in the state legislature. The next year he gained appointment as the local postmaster. In 1834 he won election to the legislature as a candidate of the new Whig Party. Soon he became a Whig leader in the state *and* passed the bar exam. In 1836 he easily won reelection to the legislature. The following year he moved to Springfield (which became the state capital in 1839) and began practicing law. Elected twice more to the legislature, he had an influential role in that body until 1842.[8] By then he had become convinced that success in politics required careful attention to constituent prejudices and not expressing unpopular views regarding race.

* * *

The Whig Party had a key role in Lincoln's career, thought, and relationship to abolitionism. The party functioned within what is known as the Second American Party System. This system replaced the First American Party System, which had consisted of the elitist nationalist Federalist Party and the agrarian state rights Republican Party. The first system had begun during the 1790s and ended in the 1810s with the collapse of the Federalist Party. Then, during the late 1810s and the 1820s, the Republican Party split in two. National Republicans, led by Henry Clay and John Quincy Adams, who was from Massachusetts, advocated a modernizing program of government aid to industry, improvements in transportation, and a national bank. This program appealed to former Federalists, commercial interests, and upwardly mobile men such as Lincoln. It did not appeal to small farmers, urban workers, and most slaveholders. These groups became supporters of the Democratic-Republican Party, which soon became the Democratic Party. In 1828 the Democrats elected Andrew Jackson, a Tennessee slaveholder, to the presidency and gained control of Congress. As president, Jackson pursued policies designed to destroy the National Bank, lessen national government power over the economy, increase the political power of poorer white men in the North, and remove American Indians from the Southeast. Jackson and his party promoted proslavery interests while discouraging an extreme southern state rights agenda.[9]

In opposition to Jackson's policies, the National Republican Party reorganized as the Whig Party in 1834. As mentioned in the introduction, Whigs represented propertied classes and the upwardly mobile. Especially in the northeastern states and Ohio, the Whigs also claimed to represent Christian morality in politics. This commitment grew out of a religious revival known as the Second Great Awakening. At camp meetings preachers assured those assembled that all people could gain salvation for their souls. They called for action to spread the faith and help the downtrodden. As a result the Awakening produced a variety of benevolent organizations designed to convert sinners and help others.[10]

* * *

As the American Party System changed, so did the abolition movement. From the 1780s into the 1820s abolitionist leaders tended to be members of a political elite. They emphasized practical, often gradual, plans for ending slavery in their states or the nation. They did not permit African Americans to join their organizations. In historian Merton L. Dillon's words, "most opponents of slavery before 1830 took for granted its political aspects and assumed it could be ended by political means." The American Colonization Society (ACS), formed in Washington, D.C., in 1816 represented an extreme form of this outlook. The ACS leaders, including Lincoln's hero Henry Clay, sought a broadly acceptable method to deal with what they regarded as the national sin of slavery. They believed they could encourage gradual emancipation in the United States by colonizing former slaves in West Africa. This, they contended, would alleviate white fears that emancipation would create an uncontrollable free black population in this country. Colonizationists also claimed that migration of former American slaves to Africa would promote conversion to Christianity on that continent. As Lincoln matured and entered politics, his background, racial prejudices, and admiration for Clay predisposed him to regard the ACS plan as a sensible solution to a slavery issue that threatened to divide the country.[11]

Some African Americans also advocated black colonization in Africa and other locations beyond U.S. borders. As early as 1773 a group of African Americans, seeking liberation from slavery in Massachusetts, pledged that upon gaining freedom they would "transport [them]selves to some part of the Coast of Africa." In 1787 black abolitionist Prince Hall of Boston and several others petitioned the Massachusetts legislature for aid in such a venture. These appeals and the colonization efforts undertaken during the first two decades of the nineteenth century by shipowner Paul Cuffe, who was of African and American Indian descent, reflected poor prospects for black success in the United States and an early form of black nationalism. But, by the time of Cuffe's death in 1817, most African American leaders opposed the ACS. They regarded the United States as their people's native land, where they should enjoy citizenship rights. Most of them asserted that the ACS aimed to *strengthen* slavery by removing its free black opponents. The brutal methods the Jackson administration employed during the 1830s to remove American Indians from southern states to western territories intensified the black leaders' outlook by raising the possibility that African Americans might also be forcefully removed.[12]

It took ten years for the African American characterizations of the ACS as proslavery to impact white abolitionists. The process occurred within the context of the Second Great Awakening and the emerging Second American Party System. During much of the 1820s young white men who opposed slavery for moral reasons supported the ACS. Among them were western–New York landowner Gerrit Smith, New York City businessmen Arthur and Lewis Tappan, and former Alabama slaveholder James G. Birney. Influenced by revivalism, Christian benevolence, and black abolitionists, they regarded slavery to be a sin and crime for which all Americans shared guilt. They, and a few other men and women, came to believe slavery had to be quickly ended to avoid divine punishment. This conviction, which Lincoln did not share until the Civil War years, persuaded them to break with the ACS and create new organizations. The result was a more radical abolitionist movement that demanded not gradual but *immediate* emancipation throughout the United States.[13]

William Lloyd Garrison led the way. Born four years before Lincoln, he had, like Lincoln, grown up in poverty and educated himself. But Garrison lived in moralistic Massachusetts rather than on the western frontier. He differed from Lincoln in religious fervor, engagement in reform movements, speaking and writing style, and interaction with African Americans. In 1829 Garrison, who had become a journalist in 1818, moved to slaveholding Baltimore to help Quaker abolitionist Benjamin Lundy publish the *Genius of Universal*

Emancipation newspaper. By then Garrison had begun to formulate an approach to the slavery issue that rested on a vision of racial equality. He called on white people to imagine what it would be like to be enslaved—to understand the anger many African Americans directed toward their oppressors. In Baltimore Garrison worked and lived with black abolitionists who strengthened his rejection of the ACS, which he portrayed as racist and proslavery. In Baltimore as well, Garrison read black abolitionist David Walker's *Appeal to the Colored Citizens of the World*, published in 1829. This seventy-eight-page essay supported the view that without immediate emancipation, African Americans would employ revolutionary violence to gain freedom. White fear that this might happen intensified in August 1831 when enslaved preacher Nat Turner led a short-lived but brutal revolt in Southampton County, Virginia.[14]

In December 1833 Garrison, Quaker abolitionists, and groups of evangelical abolitionists from New York City and western New York met in Philadelphia. There they formed the American Anti-Slavery Society (AASS), which became the dominant abolitionist organization of the 1830s. In addition to Garrison and many other white men, only three black men and four white women participated in this initial meeting. But these few black men and white women represented the organization's egalitarian spirit and future inclusiveness. The AASS's Declaration of Sentiments, drafted by Garrison, called for immediate general emancipation without "expatriation." It called for securing "to the colored population of the United States, all rights and privileges which belong to them as men, and as Americans." In accord with Quaker teachings, as well as in reaction to Turner's revolt, members renounced violent means and urged slaves to do likewise. They pledged to rely on "moral suasion" (appeals to Christian conscience) to spread immediatism throughout the North and into the South. During the following years the AASS expanded an existing petition campaign calling on Congress to abolish slavery in the national capital. By mid-decade the organization had begun sending massive amounts of antislavery propaganda into the South.[15]

Immediate abolitionists, through meetings, lectures, petition drives, newspapers, pamphlets, and books, had a major impact (much of it negative) on the American climate of opinion. By 1838 the AASS claimed 1,350 affiliate societies and a quarter-million members, most of whom resided in Massachusetts, New York, Ohio, and Pennsylvania. But, throughout their movement's existence, immediatists remained a tiny minority in the North. They were even more of a minority in the Border South; and they barely existed in the Lower South. In Lincoln's Illinois, they made only incremental progress during the 1830s and did best in the northern part of the state where settlers from the Northeast predominated.

Aside from Illinois' frontier conditions, several factors account for abolitionism's slowness to expand in that state. First there was the pervasive antiblack prejudice that influenced Lincoln, others from the South, and many migrants from the Northeast. Second the immediatists' radical program for ending slavery and gaining black equality, as well as the harsh language they directed toward slaveholders and those who defended slaveholders, alienated those who sought national harmony. Third the pro-southern, anti-abolitionist Democratic Party dominated Illinois. Although some Illinois residents resisted such pressures and embraced the immediatists' emotional crusade for black freedom, Lincoln did not. His reserved personality contrasted with prominent immediatists' evangelical fervor. He read the Bible and professed belief in a providential supreme being. But he never joined a church—let alone an evangelical one. Although the Second Great Awakening had reached Illinois, Lincoln maintained an austere rationalistic faith.[16]

Immediatist abolitionists during the 1830s tended to vote for Whig candidates and, where they could vote, black men did as well. Consequently some northern Whig politicians, unlike their Democratic counterparts, spoke against slavery expansion and slaveholder influence in Washington. A few northern Whig politicians, such as Ohio congressman Joshua R. Giddings, belonged at times to abolitionist organizations. This was not the case among southern Whigs. During the 1830s they ranged between extreme proslavery advocates and slavery's mild critic Henry Clay, a perennial Whig candidate for president.[17] In Illinois Lincoln at times used popular opposition to abolitionism for partisan political gain.

During the mid-to-late 1830s that opposition included violent anti-abolitionist action in the North. Racism and the fear that immediatism threatened the social order and the Union had major roles in causing the violence. Mob attacks on abolitionist speakers, newspaper offices, and meetings proliferated. Lincoln, like many politicians, responded to this anti-abolitionist spirit by charging that candidates for office whom he opposed *were* abolitionists and favored black rights. During the 1836 presidential campaign Jackson's sitting Democratic vice president Martin Van Buren of New York ran successfully for president against several Whig candidates. As the campaign progressed, Lincoln, who argued against black suffrage in Illinois, accused Van Buren of having, in 1821, favored voting rights for black men in New York. In 1840, when Van Buren who ran unsuccessfully for reelection against Indiana Whig William Henry Harrison, Lincoln and others repeated the charge that Van Buren favored black suffrage. Lincoln went so far as to claim that Van Buren "advocated and supported Abolitionist principles." Such charges are remarkable because Van Buren appealed to southern audiences and opposed the limited abolitionist goal of ending slavery in the District of Columbia.[18]

More frequently Lincoln, rather than using charges of abolitionism against his political opponents, called on abolitionists and their enemies to restrain themselves. What is striking is how cautiously he did so. One example of that caution is the mild "protest" he and fellow representative Dan Stone issued in response to the Illinois legislature's January 1837 passage, by a vote of seventy-seven to six, of what were themselves moderately proslavery and anti-abolitionist resolutions. These resolutions deplored slavery's existence "in a land of liberty." But they emphasized protecting "the right of property in slaves . . . sacred to the slave-holding States." They opposed "the formation of abolition societies and the doctrines promulgated by them." They held that Congress could not "abolish slavery in the District of Columbia, against the consent of the citizens of the District." Echoing the legislature, Lincoln and Stone held that "the institution of slavery is founded on both injustice and bad policy; but . . . the promulgation of abolition doctrine tends rather to increase than to abate its evils." They denied that Congress had the power to "interfere with the institution of slavery in the different States." They held that Congress should not "abolish slavery in the District of Columbia . . . unless at the request of the people of said District." Their words amounted to a slightly more negative characterization of slavery than the legislature's resolutions and a slightly clearer statement concerning Congress's power over slavery in the District of Columbia.[19]

Another example of Lincoln's caution regarding abolitionism is his indirect, limited, and purposefully dispassionate response to abolitionist Elijah P. Lovejoy's violent death. Elijah and his younger brother Owen Lovejoy had been born and raised in Maine. In 1827 Elijah had moved to St. Louis, Missouri, where he published his newspaper, the *Observer*. In 1833 he began criticizing slavery in the newspaper's columns. In 1836 mob actions drove him, his family, and his newspaper out of St. Louis and across the Mississippi River to Alton, Illinois. There Owen joined them. And, in October 1837, the Lovejoys, Edward Beecher of Illinois College, and Elihu Wolcott organized an Illinois branch of the AASS. In response proslavery leaders in Illinois declared abolitionism to be "at variance with Christianity" and a fanatical threat to the white South. A few weeks later a proslavery Alton mob killed Elijah as he defended his press.[20]

Abolitionists declared Elijah Lovejoy to be a martyr to their cause. Lincoln portrayed Lovejoy's death as only one example of a disturbing pattern in American society. In a speech at Springfield's Young Men's Lyceum a few months after the killing, Lincoln talked about the "wild and ferocious passions" in the United States. He said these passions threatened respect for law, "sober judgements of the courts," and civil government. He denounced mobs that "burn churches, ravage and rob provision stores, throw printing-presses into rivers, shoot editors, and hang and burn obnoxious persons at pleasure." He described the lynching of gamblers in Missouri and the burning of a "mulatto man" in St. Louis after the man had killed a constable. Lincoln did not mention Lovejoy by name or otherwise elaborate on his references to destroying newspaper presses and shooting editors. He took a neutral position regarding abolitionism. Advocating abolition was, he said, "either a right to be protected by law or a wrong to be legally prohibited, although in neither case" should "mob law" be used against it. Historian Carl F. Wieck observes that in this speech Lincoln separated himself from abolitionists *and* slavery's defenders by "treating the emotional topic of abolition in a cool logical manner."[21]

Yet Lincoln, as his later claim to have always been "naturally antislavery" suggests, did not regard slavery as a wholly abstract issue. Looking back from 1856, he recalled that between 1825 and 1827 his father had treated him as a slave, renting him out to work for others. During flatboat trips down the Mississippi River to New Orleans in 1828 and 1831 he observed a slave auction and perhaps saw slaves "chained—mutilated—whipt & scourged." Two of Lincoln's friends reported that he reacted with disgust and sadness.[22] By the end of the 1830s, as southern states demanded extradition from northern states of individuals charged with helping slaves escape, Lincoln demonstrated a degree of sympathy for abolitionists and their goals. In January 1839 he voted to postpone a resolution pending in the Illinois legislature that criticized Governor Edward Kent of Maine for refusing to extradite to Georgia two seamen accused of helping slaves escape. In early 1839 Lincoln voted with the Illinois legislature's majority against resolutions calling on Congress to reject without consideration abolitionist petitions pleading for emancipation in the District of Columbia. But, unlike a few other northerners who had witnessed the realities of slavery in the South, Lincoln did not become an abolitionist.[23]

DIFFERENT PATHS

During the 1840s the Whig Party remained united as most of its leaders, North and South, sought to deflect or compromise divisive sectional issues. And, despite losing some support among northerners, the party appeared to grow stronger as the decade passed. In contrast the abolition movement fragmented, with several of its factions becoming more radical and one becoming directly involved in electoral politics. Lincoln initially took little interest in these abolitionist developments. He did, however, begin to interact with individual abolitionists, and his views on some points converged with those represented by the movement.

The major national political issues centered on the Republic of Texas, war with Mexico, the formerly Mexican provinces of New Mexico and California, and the District of Columbia. Slaveholding Texas had gained independence from Mexico in March 1836. After years of debate Congress annexed Texas in December 1845, which led to war with Mexico in May 1846. When the United States acquired California and New Mexico as a result of the war, the status of slavery within their boundaries became a contentious issue. All abolitionists and many northern Whig politicians opposed annexation of Texas, the war, and slavery expansion into the Southwest. A few Whigs joined abolitionists in calling for ending slavery, or at least the slave trade, in the District of Columbia. These convergences increased abolitionist influence on northern Whigs generally and to a degree on Lincoln. But Lincoln's limited interest in the Texas issue, limited opposition to the war against Mexico, limited opposition to slavery expansion, and limited support for action against slavery in the district earned him little regard among abolitionists.

* * *

The mob violence that Lincoln had condemned in 1837 continued to impact abolitionists. Waves of anti-abolitionist, antiblack, and proslavery riots occurred across the North. These riots and the failure of moral suasion to change popular opinion in either the North or South contributed to the AASS's splintering at its May 1840 annual meeting. The philosophical, strategic, and tactical differences among the various abolitionist factions also contributed to the organization's breakup. The breakup in turn helped produce more aggressive abolitionist postures toward slavery and the South.[1]

Garrison and his mostly New Englander associates retained control of a much diminished AASS. In response to the mob violence and lack of progress in the North, they had come to regard slavery as only the worst of the nation's many sins and crimes. Therefore, in addition to demanding immediate emancipation, they advocated women's rights. They called for withdrawal from churches that communed with slaveholders. They endorsed nonresistance, a form of pacifistic anarchism that condemned all government that relied on force. In 1843 the Garrisonians declared the U.S. Constitution to be irrevocably proslavery and demanded "No Union with Slaveholders," meaning that the northern states must secede from the Union. Though often professed pacifists, Garrison and his associates predicted that this would lead to a massive slave revolt that white southerners could not on their own put down.[2]

A second abolitionist faction, centered in New York City and extending to small groups throughout the North and Border South, called on abolitionists to work through the nation's churches rather than withdraw from them. Led by Lewis Tappan, these evangelicals regarded Garrisonian disunionism as abandonment of the slaves. Working through the American Missionary Association, they supported abolitionist preachers in the Border and Middle South and continued to send abolitionist propaganda into the South.[3] To Tappan's west, in New York's intensely evangelized Burned-Over District, a third faction arose. Best known as radical political abolitionists (RPAs), and led by Gerrit Smith, the faction (contrary to Garrisonians) interpreted the U.S. Constitution as an antislavery document that made slavery illegal throughout the country—including within the slave-labor states. Slaves, RPAs asserted, had a legal right to escape from their masters, and abolitionists had a duty to go into the South to help them.

When RPAs formed the initially abolitionist Liberty Party in 1840, a fourth more moderate and much larger abolitionist faction joined them. This faction, though centered in the border city of Cincinnati, had supporters scattered throughout the North. Led by journalist Gamaliel Bailey and pious non-abolitionist attorney Salmon P. Chase, its members rejected both the Garrisonian and the RPA interpretations of the Constitution. Instead they endorsed a more conventional interpretation, shared by northern Whigs, some northern Democrats, and, to a degree, Lincoln. This interpretation held that neither the U.S. government nor the northern states could legitimately interfere with slavery where it existed in the southern states. But it also held that Congress could abolish slavery in the District of Columbia and the territories, repeal the Fugitive Slave Law of 1793, end the interstate slave trade, and otherwise discourage slavery within the national domain. The moderate Liberty abolitionists aimed to end slavery in the South by expanding their organization into that section. During the 1840s they made meagre progress toward that goal in the border slave states of Kentucky and Maryland.[4]

* * *

As Lincoln campaigned in 1840 for Whig presidential candidate William Henry Harrison, and accused Democratic candidate Martin Van Buren of being an abolitionist, he ignored the Liberty Party and its presidential candidate James G. Birney. Birney, who as editor of the abolitionist *Philanthropist* newspaper withstood a mob attack in Cincinnati, had no chance to receive more than a few thousand votes in the election. And not until 1845 did Lincoln mention the Liberty Party in his correspondence. That came when Putnam County,

Illinois, "Liberty-man" Williamson Durley proposed to Lincoln that Whiggish Liberty Party supporters and "whigs proper" unite.

Lincoln welcomed Durley's suggestion of political cooperation. But he lectured Durley regarding the negative impact of Birney's second Liberty Party presidential candidacy on the outcome of the 1844 election. Lincoln contended (with considerable accuracy) that Birney, by attracting a minority of Whig voters in New York, had deprived Whig candidate Henry Clay of the state's electoral vote. That in turn, Lincoln suggested, brought about the election of un-equivocally proslavery Democrat James K. Polk of Tennessee to the presidency. Alluding vaguely to Clay's wavering opposition to Texas annexation, Lincoln held that Durley's New York counterparts should have voted for Clay because Polk would certainly annex Texas. Lincoln regarded the Liberty Party's principled position of not doing "*evil* that *good* may come" as naïve. He advised Durley that residents of the North had a "duty . . . due to the Union of the states . . . to let slavery of the other states alone."[5]

Earlier Lincoln had begun a closer, more extended and ambiguous relationship with Illinois abolitionists in regard to aiding fugitive slaves. By 1841 an underground railroad slave-escape network had reached the Springfield area. Unlike some politicians who later became Republicans, Lincoln did not physically aid escapees. But he provided financial support. In 1843 abolitionist Luther N. Ransom, who had been born in the Burned-Over District and moved to the Springfield area during the early 1830s, told another abolitionist that Lincoln "always helps me when I call upon him for a man that is arrested as a runaway." Two decades later abolitionist journalist Zebina Eastman of Chicago remarked similarly. But, unlike abolitionist lawyers and (once again) unlike several politicians who became Republicans, Lincoln did not represent fugitive slaves in court. Instead he represented at least one slaveholder in court against abolitionists. This occurred in 1847 when two Coles County, Illinois, abolitionists helped a black woman and her children escape from a Kentucky master who had illegally held them as slaves in Illinois. When the master sued the abolitionists for damages, both the master and one of the abolitionists asked Lincoln to serve as his attorney. Largely because the master asked first, Lincoln chose to represent him—and went on to lose the case decisively.[6]

* * *

Lincoln, during the 1840s, clearly did not share abolitionists' level of moral antagonism to slavery.[7] Even in regard to the issue of slavery's territorial expansion, where sectional, political, economic, and demographic self-interest might have inclined Lincoln to take a firm stand, he demonstrated more flexibility than abolitionists and some of his fellow northern Whigs. His nationalism, ties to southern Whigs, and what he perceived to be in the best interests of his political career (rather than the slavery issue) determined his course.

When he lectured Williamson Durley concerning the Liberty Party's alleged role in allowing the annexation of Texas to take place, Lincoln added that he had "never [been] . . . much interested in the Texas question." He "never could very clearly see how the annexation would augment the evil of slavery." This was, he asserted, because masters would take slaves to Texas whether or not the United States annexed it. Lincoln's neutral outlook contrasted with that of abolitionists, particularly that of Benjamin Lundy. As soon as Texas gained independence, Lundy, then living in Philadelphia, published articles warning the North against annexation of this huge slaveholding republic. Lundy also traveled to Washington to lobby former president John Quincy Adams, who had become a Whig congressman from Massachusetts, in opposition to annexation. Adams in turn led an effort that helped delay the admission of Texas to the Union until December 1845.[8]

By May 1846, as Lincoln launched what became a successful campaign to be elected to Congress, Texas's admission had led (as Adams and others predicted) to war with Mexico. The spark came when President Polk sent an American army commanded by General Zachary Taylor into Mexican territory beyond what had been Texas's traditional southwestern boundary. Polk and other American imperialists hoped to use the war to acquire an expanded version of Texas, plus New Mexico and California. Immediately abolitionists and some northern Whigs, including most prominently Adams and

Ohio congressman Joshua R. Giddings, denounced the war as part of a southern plot to expand slavery and consolidate slaveholder control of the U.S. government. In contrast Lincoln, realizing that an expression of antislavery views could hurt his chances for election, did not discuss slavery during his campaign that summer and fall.[9]

Lincoln's victory in the election ended his ability to avoid the slavery issue. But it was Henry Clay's moderate border state perspective, rather than the abolitionists' more vehement views regarding the war and slavery, that shaped Lincoln's outlook as he began his congressional term in December 1847. Five years earlier Lincoln had wed Mary Todd, who in 1839 moved to Springfield from Lexington, Kentucky, where her prominent slaveholding family continued to reside. As the Lincolns traveled east from Springfield to Washington during the fall of 1847, they spent three weeks with the Todd family in Lexington. There Lincoln heard Clay speak against the war. Polk, Clay charged, had begun it "for the purpose of propagating slavery." Simultaneously Clay defended the right of each state to decide by itself the issue of slavery within its bounds.[10]

Clay's moderate views greatly influenced Lincoln's course in Congress. They did so despite Lincoln's decision to lodge in Washington at Anna Sprigg's boardinghouse, where he came into contact with fellow-boarder Giddings. Sprigg's establishment had become known as the "Abolition House" because from the late 1830s into the early 1840s abolition lobbyists Joshua Leavitt and Theodore Weld (both based in New York City) had boarded at Sprigg's with Giddings and other antislavery congressmen. By the time Lincoln arrived, Leavitt and Weld were gone and the "Abolition House" name no longer applied, despite Giddings's continued residence. And, although Giddings respected him, Lincoln did not share Giddings's association with abolitionists, radical opposition to the war against Mexico, and staunch resistance to slavery expansion.[11]

Instead, compared to all abolitionist factions, Giddings, and a few other antislavery congressmen, Lincoln expressed views regarding the war that were even more moderate than Henry Clay's. Garrisonians portrayed the war as an example of slavery's corrupting impact on the nation and demanded dissolution of the Union. RPA Gerrit Smith declared the war to be "the most diabolical of all wars." He suggested that "the American people fall upon their knees to seek from God and Mexico forgiveness." Liberty journalist Gamaliel Bailey, who had moved from Cincinnati to Washington to edit the *National Era* newspaper, described the war as robbery and murder aimed at forcing slavery into free Mexican territory. In Congress Giddings called it "a war of aggression and conquest" motivated by "a desire to extend and sustain an institution on which the curse of the Almighty most visibly rests."[12]

Lincoln in his "Spot Resolutions," which he presented in the House of Representatives in December 1847, criticized Polk for provoking the war *without* criticizing the war itself. The following month Lincoln voted in favor of a resolution declaring the war to have been "unnecessarily and unconstitutionally commenced by the President." But, when Lincoln spoke against Polk's conduct, he did not mention slavery. In June 1848 in a speech in Wilmington, Delaware, he said "he did not believe . . . that this war was originated for the purpose of extending slave territory." And, unlike Giddings and a few other antiwar Whigs, Lincoln always voted in favor of appropriation bills to pay for the war. When Democrat Usher F. Linder wrote to Lincoln from Illinois linking Whigs who opposed the war to abolitionists, Lincoln denied the charge. How, he asked, could southern Whigs in the House who regarded the war as "'unnecessary and unconstitutional'" be called abolitionists? That July Lincoln distinguished between opposing how Polk had begun the war and supporting successful execution of it. He praised the men who served. He commended Whig presidential candidate Taylor, who commanded them, for bringing the war "to a speedy and honorable termination."[13]

Two years earlier, during the congressional session that preceded the one in which Lincoln served, Pennsylvania Democrat David Wilmot had introduced a proviso, which called for banning slavery in territories that might be gained from Mexico as a result of the war. Like Lincoln, Wilmot was no abolitionist. Instead Wilmot only desired to protect the interests of free white labor in the territories and the North. The House passed the Wilmot Proviso that August and passed it again in February 1847. Each time the Senate defeated it. Although Lincoln was not in Congress at these times, during his term he voted at least twice in favor of similar legislation, which also failed to become law. These votes, for the first time, placed Lincoln on record as opposing slavery expansion. They convinced his colleagues that he was at best a reliable vote against such expansion. In September 1849 the non-abolitionist *New-York Daily Tribune* described Lincoln as a "strong but judicious enemy of slavery." Years later, Giddings's son-in-law George W. Julian recalled Lincoln to have been, during his term in Congress, "a moderate Wilmot Proviso man," whose "anti-slavery education had scarcely begun."[14]

* * *

Lincoln also acted judiciously in regard to attempts, initiated during the 1820s by abolitionists and a few northern Whigs, to end slavery and the slave trade in the District of Columbia. During his first month in Congress, Lincoln supported Giddings as the Ohioan pressed this issue. And, during the first half of 1848, Lincoln witnessed events that might have strengthened his support for emancipation in the district, given his expressed dislike of slavery and mob violence. That January "three ruffians" seized an enslaved black man named Henry Wilson who worked as a waiter at Sprigg's. Shortly thereafter the kidnappers placed Wilson in a slave prison pending sale south. When Giddings submitted a resolution calling for a congressional investigation into the kidnapping, Lincoln backed him. But, unlike several other Sprigg boarders, Lincoln did not actively join in Giddings's successful effort to secure Wilson's freedom.[15]

Similarly that April, when seventy-seven slaves unsuccessfully attempted to escape from Washington on the schooner *Pearl*, Lincoln did not become involved in the controversy that followed. RPA William L. Chaplin, who served as the Washington correspondent for several New York newspapers, had helped plan the escape attempt. Giddings and Bailey had prior knowledge that the mass escape would take place. As proslavery riots ensued, the two men stood at the center of the controversy and faced physical threats. Independent Democratic senator John P. Hale of New Hampshire and Whig congressman John G. Palfrey of Massachusetts, both of whom had abolitionist ties, spoke on Giddings's and Bailey's behalf. Lincoln remained silent.[16]

Thereafter Lincoln followed a conservative, rather than moderate, course regarding slavery in the District of Columbia. In December 1848 he joined a small minority of northern Whigs who voted against Palfrey's bill to abolish slavery there. Lincoln objected to the bill because it did not provide compensation to masters. A few days later he voted against Giddings's inflammatory call for a referendum, in which black men could vote, on slavery in the district. During that December and the following January Lincoln voted several times against Whig representative Daniel Gott's resolution calling for ending the slave trade in the district.[17]

On January 10, 1849, Lincoln drafted a bill of his own in regard to gradual and compensated emancipation in the district. It provided for a referendum on the issue in which only "free white male citizen[s]" could participate. It also stipulated that local authorities would have continuing power "to provide active and efficient means to arrest and deliver up to their owners, all fugitive slaves escaping into said District." Lincoln, who later claimed his "former backers" had abandoned him, did not formally introduce this bill, despite Giddings's willingness to support it as a compromise measure. As a result abolitionists failed *at the time* to notice Lincoln's proposal. However, over a decade later as Lincoln began his campaign to be elected U.S. president, his proposed bill served as the basis for a famously negative abolitionist characterization of him. Garrisonian orator Wendell Phillips of Boston called Lincoln "the slave-hound of Illinois." Phillips described Lincoln's decade old proposal as "one of the poorest and most confused specimens of pro-slavery compromise."[18]

* * *

It was Lincoln's conservative nationalism that led him to differ so markedly from abolitionists in regard to Texas, the war against Mexico, and emancipation in the District of Columbia. Similarly, even as he became more publicly opposed to slavery expansion, his staunch identification with the Whig Party predisposed him to view 1848's presidential politics quite differently than abolitionists did. Even before Lincoln entered Congress in December 1847, he had, for partisan reasons, decided to support slaveholding general Zachary Taylor for the 1848 Whig presidential nomination. He believed Taylor could be elected, help other Whigs gain state and national office, and thereby open many government jobs to Whig office-seekers. When Lincoln arrived in Washington, he joined a mostly southern group of congressmen, known as the "Young Indians" to promote Taylor's candidacy.[19] Abolitionists, of course, would not promote a slaveholder's candidacy. Garrisonians pledged to vote for *no* candidate who sought office under what they regarded as the proslavery U.S. Constitution. Members of other abolitionist factions would vote only for fellow abolitionists or steadfastly antislavery candidates.

In 1848 a minority of northern Whigs, including Giddings, pledged to support only a presidential candidate who opposed the further expansion of slavery. Such Whigs, centered in Ohio and Massachusetts, united with a similarly inclined minority of northern Democrats, centered in New York, and with the moderate Liberty faction. They met in Buffalo that August to form the Free Soil Party with the Wilmot Proviso as its platform and former Democratic president Martin Van Buren as its candidate for president.[20] Because of this limited platform and because Van Buren had long defended slavery, the Free Soil Party fell far short of abolitionism. Even so the Free Soilers appealed to northern antislavery sentiment better than either the Democratic Party or the Whig Party could. The Democrats and their candidate for president, Lewis Cass of Michigan, proposed to allow settlers in each territory to decide whether or not to permit slavery. The Whigs, who as Lincoln had hoped, nominated Taylor, took no stand on the issue.[21]

Lincoln attended the Whig national convention held in Philadelphia in June, campaigned for Taylor, and criticized the Free Soilers. In his speeches he said he believed that if Congress passed the Wilmot Proviso, Taylor (based on the Whig principle of legislative supremacy) would not veto it. In addition Lincoln advised those inclined to vote Free Soil that, while Van Buren could not be elected, he could draw votes from Taylor and produce a victory for Cass and other Democrats who would encourage slavery expansion. In a speech at Worcester, Massachusetts, Lincoln stressed opposition to slavery extension, without suggesting that preventing such extension would be a step toward emancipation in the southern states. In a statement that ran contrary to abolitionist views, he declared, "All agreed that slavery was an evil, but that we [northerners] were not responsible for it and cannot affect it in the States of this union where we do not live." He added that he believed Massachusetts residents placed too much importance on the issue of slavery in the South. As the election approached, Illinois Democrat Murray McConnel ridiculed Lincoln's attempt to convince Free Soilers to vote for a candidate such as Taylor who owned "three hundred negro slaves."[22]

Abolitionists, all of whom took no notice of Lincoln's 1848 speeches, made remarks similar to McConnel's regarding the Taylor candidacy. But abolitionists differed among themselves regarding the Free Soil Party. Church-oriented abolitionist Lewis Tappan "felt stabbed in the vitals" by those Liberty leaders, such as Salmon P. Chase, who supported Van Buren. Tappan, and less than three thousand others, voted for Gerrit Smith as the candidate of what remained of the Liberty Party. Politically active Quaker abolitionist poet John Greenleaf Whittier similarly regarded Free Soil as a compromise of abolitionist principles that could lead to more compromises. In contrast Garrison and preeminent black abolitionist Frederick Douglass asserted that growing abolitionist influence had led to the Free Soil Party. Following Taylor's victory and a good performance on the part of the Free Soilers, who elected fourteen congressmen, Garrison wrote privately, "As for the 'Free Soil' movement, I am for backing it as a cheering sign of the times." He regarded the new party as "an immutable proof of the progress we have made, under God, in changing public sentiment." As for Lincoln's "Whig Taylor party," Garrison called for "expend[ing] . . . our heaviest ammunition" against it. Douglass, who had attended the Free Soil convention, reacted more cautiously than Garrison to the new party, but hardly so negatively as Lincoln had. Assessing in May 1849 "what good" the Free Soil Party had done, Douglass noted its having "rallied a large number of the people of the North in apparent hostility to the whole system of American slavery." He believed the party had "rebuked and humbled quite a number of corrupt and cringing politicians." He hoped it had "checked the proud and arrogant pretensions of the slaveholder with respect to the extension of slavery."[23]

Lincoln did not think in such terms during 1848 and 1849. Rather than regard slavery and opposition to it as matters of principle, he continued to approach them as distractions to be avoided and finessed. Rather than regard Free Soil as a compromise of principle, as did Tappan and Whittier, Lincoln saw it as threat to Whig Party strength at the polls. Rather than perceive Free Soil as a political product of northern antislavery sentiment, as did Douglass and Garrison, he portrayed it as leading to slavery expansion under a Democratic administration. Most important, based on his obsession with patronage following Taylor's victory and the end of his brief time in Congress, Lincoln perceived Free Soil as a threat to his being able to find jobs for others and himself under a Whig administration.[24]

LIMITED CONVERGENCE

A braham Lincoln had been out of Congress for over a year when, in September 1850, that body passed the last of the bills included in the Compromise of 1850. Lincoln's hero Henry Clay had put the Compromise together and Lincoln's political archenemy Stephen A. Douglas had maneuvered its provisions through the legislative process. Aimed to end North-South discord, the Compromise favored the North by admitting California to the Union as a free-labor state and requiring slaveholding Texas to give up its claim to eastern New Mexico. Otherwise it favored the South. It gave slavery a chance to expand into New Mexico and Utah Territories. It kept slavery (but not the slave trade) legal in the District of Columbia. It instituted stronger U.S. government support for masters seeking to recover slaves who had escaped to the North. This last measure, known as the Fugitive Slave Law of 1850, came in response to rising numbers of slave escapes and fear among white southerners that such escapes undermined slavery in the Border South. It authorized U.S. marshals to help apprehend escapees, denied jury trials to alleged fugitives, appointed special federal commissioners to adjudicate cases, and made it a federal crime to help slaves escape.[1]

Lincoln and most Americans, North and South, welcomed the Compromise provisions as a means of saving the Union and preventing sectional war. But slavery's strongest advocates demanded government protection for slavery in all U.S. territories. They also predicted that the Fugitive Slave Law of 1850 would not be enforced.

Meanwhile Free Soilers and those northern Whigs and Democrats most opposed to slavery expansion continued to call on Congress to ban slavery from all territories. Abolitionists opposed all the proslavery Compromise measures and pledged physical resistance to the Fugitive Slave Law.[2]

In a eulogy for President Taylor, who died before the Compromise measures became law, Lincoln agreed with the compromisers' goals. And, supposing incorrectly that Taylor had supported the Compromise, he said, "I fear the one *great* question of the day, is not now so likely to be partially acquiesced in by the different sections of the Union, as it would have been, could Gen. Taylor have been spared to us." Otherwise Lincoln did not immediately become involved in the post-Compromise dispute. Instead, from 1851 to 1853, he worked, in conjunction with his law partner William Herndon, to revive and expand his legal practice.[3]

Of all the Compromise measures, the Fugitive Slave Law presented the greatest difficulty for Lincoln and revealed an inconsistency between his political and personal views. On the one hand he refused to act as an attorney on behalf of fugitive slaves because he feared becoming "party to a violation of the . . . Law." In one of his few 1852 campaign speeches in favor of Whig presidential candidate Winfield Scott, he went so far as to charge Democratic candidate Franklin Pierce with opposing the law. On the other hand he privately declared the law to be "very obnoxious" and "ungodly." In regard to fugitive slaves, Lincoln confessed in 1855 to his proslavery Kentucky friend Joshua Speed, "I hate to see the poor creatures hunted down, and caught, and carried back to their stripes, and unrewarded toils; but I bite my lip and keep quiet."[4]

* * *

As pro-Compromise sentiment dominated American politics and thought during the early 1850s, the abolitionist movement suffered a brief relapse similar to that suffered by Lincoln's political career. "Union" meetings proliferated and mob attacks on abolitionists revived. Membership in abolitionist organizations declined, as did abolitionist newspapers' circulation. In 1852 the Whig and Democratic national platforms pledged to oppose further antislavery agitation. But abolitionism rebounded as many black and white northerners physically resisted the Fugitive Slave Law. Harriet Beecher Stowe's *Uncle Tom's Cabin*, a novel that dramatized the fugitive slaves' plight, encouraged large segments of northern public opinion to support such action. When abolitionists who rescued fugitive slaves from custody faced indictment, prosecution, and imprisonment, few northern juries convicted them. Northern state legislatures passed laws designed to discourage recapture of slaves and prevent kidnapping of free African Americans.[5]

Physical resistance to slave renditions centered in New England, western New York, and northeastern Ohio. In Illinois little such resistance occurred outside of Chicago, and Lincoln's antislavery views remained moderate. In his eulogy for Henry Clay, which he delivered in Springfield on July 6, 1852, Lincoln portrayed Clay as a nationalist who recognized both northern and southern interests and who, through his compromise proposals in 1820 and 1850, saved the Union from disruption over "the slavery question." According to Lincoln, abolitionists contrasted with Clay. He described them as "those who would shiver into fragments the Union of these States; tear to tatters its now venerated constitution; and even burn the last copy of the Bible, rather than slavery should continue a single hour." In regard to anti-abolitionist words and actions, Lincoln asserted that abolitionists had "received, and are receiving their just execration."[6]

Lincoln, following Clay's example, also denounced those who "for the sake of perpetuating slavery" assailed the Declaration of Independence, which he characterized ambiguously as "the white-man's charter of freedom—the declaration that 'all men are created free and equal.'" He opposed reopening the Atlantic slave trade, upheld the goal of "ultimate emancipation," and warned that slavery's strongest defenders threatened to extinguish the example America set for the world. He then endorsed Clay's prescription for defusing the slavery issue: the expatriation of emancipated black people to the American Colonization Society's Liberia colony in West Africa. Often relying on Clay's 1827 speech on behalf of that organization, Lincoln argued that, unlike abolitionists, advocates of colonization did not threaten to bring about a "great moral revolution." The American Colonization Society (ACS) did not encourage slaves "to weaken their obligations of obedience" or threaten a master's right to his "property." Rather, according to Lincoln, the ACS program would increase the monetary value of slaves who remained in the United States. It would "relieve slave-holders from the troublesome presence of the free negroes." And former American slaves would carry to Africa the "fruits of religion, civilization, law and liberty." Lincoln liked the ACS's gradualism and claimed the organization had gained strength in each year since Clay's 1827 speech. In regard to the separation of the races Lincoln declared, "May it indeed be realized!"[7]

Lincoln retained these views regarding colonization for many years. He addressed the ACS's Illinois branch in 1853 and 1855. He served on its board of managers in 1858. He thereby placed himself at odds with all existing abolitionist organizations, as well as with the most prominent abolitionists. A few months before Clay died, Garrison wrote of him, "There is no man living, who has done so much for the extension and perpetuation of slavery . . . or who is more inimical to the anti-slavery movement." Garrison pointed out that "Southern slaveholders and their Northern allies" had organized the ACS "for the expatriation of the free colored population of this country to Africa, *on account of their freedom and complexion*." He noted the organization's racist depictions of African Americans, including its reference to them as an "inferior race, repugnant to our republican (!) feelings, and dangerous to our republican (!) institutions." Frederick Douglass called the ACS "an old enemy of the colored people of this country." According to Douglass, the ACS assumed incorrectly that racial "prejudice can never be overcome" and could be avoided only "by . . . removing us to Liberia."[8]

Yet Lincoln, during the 1850s, did not diverge radically from a minority of abolitionists regarding colonization. That minority supported black expatriation as its members despaired of achieving emancipation and equal rights for African Americans in the United States. The Fugitive Slave Law led white abolitionist James G. Birney and black abolitionist Martin R. Delany, among others, to advocate a better life for black people beyond America's borders. In 1852 Delany wrote,

"There have been people in all ages under certain circumstances, that may be benefitted by emigration . . . and . . . there are circumstances under which emigration is absolutely necessary to their political elevation." As prospects for peaceful emancipation in the South declined during the late 1850s, such stalwart abolitionists as Gerrit Smith and Theodore Parker praised border slave state Republicans Francis P. Blair Sr. and Francis P. Blair Jr.'s plan for federally supported, voluntary black colonization in Central America.[9]

* * *

Neither resistance to the Fugitive Slave Law nor disputes over colonization drew Lincoln back into politics during the mid-1850s. Instead Stephen A. Douglas's introduction of his Nebraska Bill into the U.S. Senate in January 1854 had this effect. The following May the bill became the Kansas-Nebraska Act. It repealed the Missouri Compromise's prohibition of slavery north of the 36°30′ line of latitude in the remaining territorial portions of the Louisiana Purchase. And it opened Kansas and Nebraska Territories to slavery by allowing male settlers to decide by majority vote, under the doctrine of popular sovereignty, whether or not to permit slavery.

In the Northeast Garrisonians and radical political abolitionists (RPAs) reacted to the Kansas-Nebraska Act in various ways. But they all emphasized the larger context of slavery's existence in the United States. Soon after Douglas introduced his bill, Garrison, speaking at New York City's Broadway Tabernacle, moved from a brief discussion of the bill to advocating universal black liberation. He received applause as he criticized opposition to slavery expansion that did not also call on masters in the South to immediately free their slaves. That fall, speaking in Chicago, Frederick Douglass (now an RPA) discussed the slavery expansion issue in more detail. But, like Garrison, he emphasized the larger issue. The United States, he warned, "will never be at peace with God until it shall, practically and universally, embrace" every human being's "right to freedom." For Douglass, Gerrit Smith, and other RPAs, this meant increased support for physical action against slavery. Smith (who had been a member of Congress during the Nebraska Bill debates and resigned shortly after the bill became law) lost hope for "a bloodless termination of American slavery." Lewis Tappan, who previously emphasized religious appeals, joined RPAs in declaring the "illegality and unconstitutionality of American slavery."[10]

As abolitionists linked the Kansas-Nebraska Act to their wider campaign against slavery, non-abolitionist Free Soilers, Wilmot Proviso Democrats, and antislavery Whigs came together to form the Republican Party. Although few Free Soilers had been abolitionists, some of them had abolitionist ties that influenced how they portrayed the Kansas-Nebraska Act and the nature of its threat. Most prominent among those who had such ties was Salmon P. Chase, who, in 1849, became a Democratic U.S. senator from Ohio. Chase had defended fugitive slaves in court, had been affiliated with Liberty abolitionists, and had served on the board of Tappan's abolitionist American and Foreign Anti-Slavery Society. Unlike Lincoln, Chase also maintained an extensive correspondence with abolitionists. In January 1854 Chase's "Appeal of the Independent Democrats in Congress to the People of the United States" portrayed the Nebraska Bill as part "of an atrocious plot" to extend slavery in violation of the Founders' and the Missouri Compromise's goals of containing slavery. The "Appeal" also endorsed the abolitionist dictum "to behold in every man a brother." It denounced slavery itself as "legalized oppression and systematized injustice." It pronounced "the cause of human freedom" to be "the cause of God."[11]

Chase's views influenced Lincoln. But three less prominent opponents of the Kansas-Nebraska Act, who had longer and more intense abolitionist associations than Chase, more directly shaped Lincoln's antislavery politics. These three, Ichabod Codding, Zebina Eastman, and Owen Lovejoy, initiated efforts toward forming the Illinois Republican Party, and in doing so, they shaped the circumstances in which Lincoln joined this party. Codding, born in New York, had served in a band of evangelical abolitionist speakers, led by Theodore Weld, during the 1830s. He had been vice president of the first Liberty convention in 1840. He promoted the party in New England and the Old Northwest, and he accepted the RPA interpretation of the U.S. Constitution. Eastman, born in Massachusetts, had helped

Benjamin Lundy edit the *Genius of Universal Emancipation* during Lundy's last years. He supported the Liberty Party in his Chicago *Western Citizen* newspaper and became a Free Soiler in 1848. Lovejoy in 1837 had joined his brother Elijah in organizing the Illinois branch of the American Anti-Slavery Society. He served as the organization's manager between 1838 and 1840. He belonged to the Liberty national committee in 1847 and aided fugitive slaves. Evangelical Christianity motivated all three of these men, and they encouraged Lincoln's increased references to religion as he began to speak against the Kansas-Nebraska Act.[12]

When Codding and Lovejoy organized, and Eastman's newspaper (renamed the *Free West*) promoted, a meeting in Springfield during early October 1854 to create an Illinois Republican Party, Lincoln did not attend. He recognized slavery's threat to "the principle of free government." He continued to express sympathy for African Americans. He described slavery as "the foulest curse." But he feared abolitionist radicalism would predominate at the meeting. He also hoped to be elected to the U.S. Senate when the state legislature met the following January. Therefore he did not want to alienate Whigs. His reluctance to challenge the slaveholders' supposed right to human property also separated him from Codding, Eastman, and Lovejoy. And, although Codding and Lovejoy were much more flexible than Garrison, Douglass, and Smith, their meeting produced resolutions that *were* radical compared to Lincolns' views. They recognized Congress's power "to prohibit slavery in *all* territories." They asserted that alleged fugitive slaves had a right to jury trials and habeas corpus.[13]

When Lincoln first spoke against the Kansas-Nebraska Act at a Whig meeting in Winchester, Illinois, in August 1854, he limited himself to opposing repeal of the Missouri Compromise and "extension of slavery into free territory." In Bloomington, Illinois, a month later, he continued to reject interference with slavery in the southern states. He acknowledged that under the Compromise of 1850 slavery might legally expand into New Mexico and Utah. He accepted that under the Missouri Compromise it might go into areas south of the 36°30' line of latitude in territorial portions of the Louisiana Purchase.[14]

It was within this context that Lincoln presented the most extensive discussion of slavery he had yet undertaken. In a speech delivered in Springfield on October 4 and then in Peoria on October 16, he portrayed slavery expansion and popular sovereignty as morally wrong and threats to *white* northerners' political and economic interests. He described slavery itself as a violation of republican principles and of a worker's right to the fruits of his labor. However, unlike abolitionists, Lincoln refused to blame white southerners for slavery's continued existence. It was a problem, he said, that could only be solved over time through colonization because white Americans would not allow African Americans to live with them in a state of equality. He continued to support the Fugitive Slave Law, with the proviso that there should be protections against using the law to enslave free people. Using the term *abolitionist* loosely, he advised his fellow Whigs to "stand WITH the abolitionist in restoring the Missouri Compromise; and stand AGAINST him when he attempts to repeal the fugitive slave law."[15]

By the time of Lincoln's Springfield and Peoria speeches, the American political situation had become very complicated and so had Lincoln's. In addition to division regarding the Kansas-Nebraska Act, a nativist movement (whose supporters became known as Know-Nothings) had a major role. This movement disrupted the northern Whig Party and led to the organization of the American Party based on anti-Catholic and anti-foreign sentiment. When local nativists asked Lincoln to be their candidate for the state legislature, he turned them down. He maintained his loyalty to the Whig Party and objected to what the American Party stood for. Shortly thereafter he accepted the local Whig organization's nomination for the same seat, although he could not serve in the legislature and be, as he desired, a candidate before the legislature for the U.S. Senate.[16]

Meanwhile, despite Lincoln's conservatism, the fledgling Illinois Republican Party, without his knowledge, appointed him to its "central committee." When in mid-November Codding requested that Lincoln attend the committee's upcoming meeting in Chicago, Lincoln did not do so. Later in a letter to Codding, Lincoln contended that no one had informed him of the appointment and he had not received the invitation until after the meeting took place. In the same letter Lincoln claimed (incorrectly) that his "opposition to the principle of slavery is as strong as that of any member of the Republican party." But he also asserted that "the *extent*" to which he felt "authorized" to act on that opposition "was . . . [not] at all satisfactory to that party." He wondered if Codding and others who had attended his Springfield speech misunderstood him or he misunderstood them.[17]

It is not surprising, therefore, that as Lincoln promoted his candidacy for the U.S. Senate, Eastman criticized him in the *Free West* as "a compromise Whig." Eastman noted that Lincoln did not oppose admitting more slave-labor states to the Union and dared not oppose the Fugitive Slave Law. But both Eastman and Lincoln were willing to adjust their perspectives. When two of Lincoln's political friends appealed to Eastman to change his stance, he traveled, along with visiting Kentucky abolitionist-cum-Republican Cassius M. Clay, to Springfield to interview Lincoln's law partner William H. Herndon. During their conversation, Herndon convinced Eastman of Lincoln's reliability regarding slavery issues. Then, on January 4, 1855, Lincoln submitted resolutions to the legislature that went beyond urging restoration of the Missouri Compromise. In these resolutions he pledged to oppose admitting either Kansas or Nebraska to the Union as a slave-labor state. He opposed slavery expansion into any territory where it did "not now legally exist." And he opposed reopening the "African slave-trade." Lincoln subsequently advised the legislature that while he would not vote to repeal the Fugitive Slave Law, he would vote to remove portions objectionable to northerners. The legislature in February 1855 nevertheless failed to elect Lincoln to the Senate, choosing instead Anti-Nebraska Democrat Lyman Trumbull.[18]

* * *

During the rest of 1855 events in Kansas Territory shaped Lincoln's and abolitionists' views regarding slavery and the Republican Party. A year earlier U.S. senator David Atchison of Missouri had decided that, to protect slavery in his state, slavery had to be established in Kansas—by force if necessary. At about the same time in Massachusetts, Eli Thayer organized the New England Emigrant Aid Company, the first of several organizations designed to promote emigration from the free-labor states to Kansas. In March illegal voters from Missouri elected a proslavery Kansas territorial legislature, which that August legalized slavery. In response "Free Staters," led by abolitionist Charles Robinson, formed military companies and acquired rifles and cannons from the Northeast. Prominent abolitionists Gerrit Smith, Thomas Wentworth Higginson, Wendell Phillips, and George L. Stearns contributed to this technically non-abolitionist undertaking. During the summer the proslavery and free-state forces in Kanas prepared for war. It broke out that November, and a few abolitionists went to Kansas to fight on the Free State side.[19]

Unlike Smith, Higginson, Phillips, Stearns, and the other abolitionists mentioned, Lincoln did not give monetary or physical support to the Free Staters. Yet the Kansas war, along with increased southern defensiveness, led him to conclude privately in August "that there is no peaceful extinction of slavery in prospect for us." He still considered himself to be a Whig, not an "abolitionist" (meaning not a Republican), and his antislavery commitment remained relatively weak. He informed his friend Speed that while he sympathized with slaves he "did no more than oppose the *extension* of slavery," particularly into Kansas Territory. He feared Kansas would become a slave-labor state, but unlike Garrison he would not seek to dissolve the Union if it did. He continued to recognize slaveholders' "legal right to the slave." He had begun to wonder (as abolitionists had before him) if the nation could "continue together *permanently— forever*—half slave and half free." But, rather than take action, he called on God to "superintend the solution."[20]

Within this moderate context Lincoln used his political contacts in central and southern Illinois and emerging eloquence to take control of the Republican movement in the state. In August 1855 he helped dissuade Lovejoy from holding a statewide organizational meeting in Springfield, arguing that the Know-Nothings had not yet weakened enough to be absorbed by "opponents of slavery extension." During that fall's state election campaign, Lincoln spoke widely in favor of restoring the Missouri Compromise and against admitting Kansas as a slave-labor state. In February 1856 he attended a meeting, held in Decatur, of Illinois newspaper editors who favored the repeal of the Kansas-Nebraska Act. He, although simply the editors' guest, influenced the meeting's resolutions in favor of restoring the Missouri Compromise and protecting foreign immigrants' rights. Other resolutions reflected those of Republican organizations in other states. They declared slavery to be local and freedom to be national. They upheld the Fugitive Slave Law. And they denied intending to interfere with slavery in the southern states.[21]

Finally the Decatur meeting appointed a committee to call an "Anti-Nebraska" state convention. Lincoln and abolitionists Codding and Lovejoy participated in that convention when it met in Bloomington on May 29. A week earlier proslavery forces had attacked the Free-State center of Lawrence, Kansas, and South Carolina congressman Preston Brooks had brutally assaulted Massachusetts's Republican senator Charles Sumner. Nevertheless Lincoln once again used his influence to produce a moderate anti-extensionist platform. He emphasized the political necessity of attracting conservative Whigs in central and southern Illinois. He told two Anti-Nebraska Democrats, "Your party is so mad at [Stephen A.] Douglas . . . that it will gulp down anything; but our [new] party . . . must not be forced to radical measures; the Abolitionists will go with us anyway."[22]

Lincoln stressed resistance to the power of slaveholders in the U.S. government and maintaining the Union, rather than confrontation in Kansas and Washington. But that did not prevent proslavery Democrats from linking him to abolitionists. Two weeks after the Bloomington convention the *Daily Illinois State Register* simultaneously ridiculed Lincoln's "timidity" *and* suggested that he shared the views of "Garrison and Fred Douglass"—the "ruling spirits of black republicanism." Assuming Lincoln was a Republican, the *Register* charged that if that party gained power it would unveil a "now suppressed platform of ultra abolitionism."[23]

* * *

At this time Garrison, Frederick Douglass, and other major abolitionist leaders still knew little if anything about Lincoln and his role in Illinois politics. Lincoln, however, *probably* had knowledge of such abolitionist leaders that went beyond stereotypical portrayals of them as fanatical advocates of disunion, race war in the South, and demolishing racial boundaries. This is because Herndon had in 1854 taken an interest in the movement and initiated a correspondence with Theodore Parker, one of the more influential (if unorthodox) abolitionist leaders. Parker, a Unitarian minister who lived in Boston, was not a Garrisonian, RPA, or evangelical. He combined support for physical action against slavery with a racist belief in Anglo-Saxon superiority. Herndon also corresponded with Garrison and Phillips. Many years later he claimed to have been an "ardent abolitionist" in 1854.[24]

Herndon had copies of the *Liberator* and equally abolitionist *National Anti-Slavery Standard*, along with the antislavery Republican *New-York Daily Tribune* and Washington *National Era* and at least two southern proslavery newspapers in the office he shared with Lincoln. Herndon also received copies of Parker's abolitionist writings, which he later claimed to have read to Lincoln along with the abolitionist newspapers. Yet Herndon shared much of Lincoln's ambivalence regarding slavery and political action against it. In early 1855 Herndon encouraged Parker to "blast slavery" and asserted that he desired "freedom and elevation of my brother man." But, as late as 1858, Herndon advised Parker that reformers must "get so low, crawl along in the mud." Historian Carl F. Wieck argues weakly that in 1854 Parker influenced Lincoln through Herndon, and that Lincoln deliberately concealed Parker's impact on him.[25] Whether or not this was the case, during the mid-1850s politically oriented Illinois abolitionists Codding, Eastman, and Lovejoy had more direct influence on Lincoln than any northeastern abolitionist leader, including Parker.

This photographic portrait shows Lincoln as he appeared in Pittsfield, Illinois, on October 1, 1858, two weeks before his final debate with Stephen A. Douglas. Courtesy of Library of Congress Prints and Photographs.

William Lloyd Garrison (1805–79) led the American Anti-Slavery Society from its founding in 1833 into the Civil War years. An advocate of the immediate abolition of slavery and equal rights for African Americans, he for many years criticized Lincoln. Courtesy of Library of Congress Prints and Photographs.

Gerrit Smith (1797–1874) was a wealthy New York landowner who led radical political abolitionists from the late 1830s into the Civil War years. A supporter of John Brown's raid on Harpers Ferry, Smith came to see great promise in Lincoln's presidency. Courtesy of Library of Congress Prints and Photographs.

Theodore Parker (1810–60) was a Unitarian minister, an intellectual associated with the Transcendentalists, and an independent
abolitionist. During the 1850s he corresponded with Lincoln's law
partner William Herndon. Courtesy of Wikimedia Commons
(original at Boston Public Library).

Frederick Douglass (1818–95), who had been
born into slavery, emerged as the leading black
abolitionist in the early 1840s. During the Civil
War Douglass criticized Lincoln while develop-
ing a personal relationship with him. Courtesy of
Library of Congress Prints and Photographs.

"THE NIGGER" IN THE WOODPILE.

This political cartoon, "'The Nigger' in the Woodpile," drawn by Louis Maurer and published by Currier and Ives in 1860, is an example of Democratic and proslavery claims that Lincoln *was* an abolitionist. At center Horace Greeley contends that the Republican Party has "no connection with the Abolition party." Instead, he says, the 1860 Republican "platform is composed entirely of rails split" by Lincoln who sits on the pile of rails. The man at left declares that he cannot be fooled because he can see "'the Nigger' peeping through the rails." Courtesy of Library of Congress Prints and Photographs.

Wendell Phillips (1811–84) was an abolitionist who, during the late 1830s, began a close association with William Lloyd Garrison. In the 1850s Phillips became America's leading orator and one of the harshest abolitionist critics of Lincoln. Courtesy of Library of Congress Prints and Photographs.

Anna Dickinson (1842–1932) was a Philadelphia Quaker who emerged during the Civil War as a young fiery abolition-ist speaker. She often denounced Lincoln. But in 1864 she also campaigned for his reelection to the presidency. Cour-tesy of Library of Congress Prints and Photographs.

This photographic print of *Watch Meeting, Dec. 31st, 1862, Waiting for the Hour,* painted by William Tolman Carlton in 1863, depicts a group of African Americans awaiting Lincoln's final Emancipation Proclamation. William Lloyd Garrison sent the original painting to Lincoln in July 1864. Courtesy of Library of Congress Prints and Photographs.

Abolitionist Sojourner Truth visited Lincoln at the White House during October 1864. In 1892 Franklin C. Courter reconstructed the visit in his painting *A. Lincoln Showing Sojourner Truth the Bible Presented by Colored People of Baltimore.* Courtesy of Library of Congress Prints and Photographs.

LINCOLN KEEPS HIS DISTANCE

As the Republican Party organized and gained power in the North, northeastern abolitionist leaders applied a policy similar to the one some of them had earlier used in regard to the Free Soil Party. They praised the new party as a step in the right direction *and* criticized it in order to prod it toward advocating immediate general emancipation. As abolitionists outside Illinois became aware of Lincoln, they extended this policy to include him. Before they did, Stephen A. Douglas and other Democrats continued their efforts to convince voters that Lincoln and Republicans generally either *were* abolitionists or had ties to the movement. The Democrats charged falsely that Lincoln, like Garrison, advocated immediate emancipation, disunion, and racial amalgamation. Meanwhile Lincoln perceived some value in abolitionist support for him and his party. But he, like others who identified with the Republicans' conservative and moderate wings, reacted guardedly toward abolitionists because he feared the political costs of being linked to them.[1]

* * *

During the 1850s the more antislavery Republicans, who sought to end slavery everywhere it existed under federal government jurisdiction (*denationalization*) as well as stop its territorial expansion, *did* have abolitionist ties. These *Radical Republicans* corresponded with abolitionists, attended abolitionist meetings, and sometimes invited abolitionists to Republican meetings. Radicals included Charles

Sumner of Massachusetts, John P. Hale of New Hampshire, William H. Seward of New York, Thaddeus Stevens of Pennsylvania, and Salmon P. Chase and Joshua R. Giddings of Ohio. In Massachusetts, Moderate Republicans, such as Henry Wilson, also interacted with abolitionists.[2]

Lincoln's words and deeds during the 1856 presidential campaign illustrate his rejection of the Radicals' example. Although he did not attend the Republican Party's first national nominating convention, which convened in Philadelphia on June 17 of that year, the anti-slavery-extension platform it adopted satisfied his limited antislavery commitment. The platform endorsed the equal rights principles of the Declaration of Independence, upheld Congress's power to prohibit slavery in territories, and contended that the Founders had sought to limit and discourage slavery. As abolitionists (most notably Frederick Douglass) pointed out, the platform *did not* oppose admitting new slave states to the Union. It *did not* call on Congress to repeal the Fugitive Slave Law of 1850 or take action against the interstate slave trade. It contained no call for emancipation in the District of Columbia.[3]

That summer and fall Lincoln campaigned throughout Illinois for Republican presidential nominee John C. Frémont, who had gained national fame as an explorer in the West and as an army officer during the war against Mexico. Lincoln also campaigned for Illinois Republican gubernatorial candidate William H. Bissell, a conservative former Democrat. Lincoln's interpretation of his party's national platform and Democratic charges that he and other Republicans were abolitionists who threatened the Union shaped his performance.

Even before the campaign began, the Democratic *Daily Illinois State Register*, published in Springfield, commented in regard to a speech Lincoln delivered there, "His niggerism has as dark a hue as that of Garrison or Fred Douglass." Later the *Register* referred to Lincoln as the "great high-priest of abolitionism." In response to such charges, Lincoln in a speech in Kalamazoo, Michigan, denied that former abolitionists who identified with the Republican Party and abolitionist praise of the party affected its policies. Referring to Democrats, Lincoln declared, "They tell us that we are in company with men who have long been known as abolitionists." He added, "What care we how many may feel disposed to labor for our cause?"[4]

In one case Lincoln *did* care. When, on July 2, Princeton, Illinois, Republicans nominated abolitionist Owen Lovejoy for Congress, Lincoln declared, "It turned me blind." Then, as he learned of Lovejoy's popularity among potential voters, Lincoln backed off. He simultaneously denied responsibility for Lovejoy's nomination and refused to cooperate with conservative Republicans who sought to replace him. Lovejoy subsequently made himself more agreeable to most Illinois Republicans, while hurting his standing among abolitionists, by agreeing that Congress could not end slavery in a state.[5]

Throughout the 1856 campaign Lincoln continued to portray his party, and its candidates, as moderate. He thereby hoped to appeal to former Whigs and current Know-Nothings, whom he urged to vote for Frémont as a means of defeating proslavery Democratic presidential candidate James Buchanan of Pennsylvania. Lincoln also claimed to be "familiar with slavery and its evils" and called for ending its expansion and slaveholder domination of the U.S. government. But he emphasized a Republican promise not to end slavery in the South. He repeatedly denied that his party favored *Garrisonian* disunionism. He attempted to shift the debate by charging that northern Democrats had ties to *southern* disunionists who regarded breaking up the Union as a means of protecting slavery. While he identified slavery as "the greatest question" before the electorate, he defined that question as "shall slavery be spread into new Territories, or not?"[6]

Abolitionists, for their part, did not neglect the issue of slavery expansion or the threat proslavery initiatives posed to white northerners' social and economic interests. And Lincoln on occasion deplored the injustices enslaved and free African Americans suffered. But usually his speeches focused on white interests in general and those of white northerners in particular. He took advantage of extreme southern defenses of slavery that portrayed it as a superior labor system suitable to be imposed on poor workers, white as well as black. In Bloomington in May 1856 he asserted that "sentiment in favor of white slavery . . . prevailed in all the slave state newspapers, except those of Kentucky, Tennessee, Missouri, and Maryland." In August he criticized the U.S. Constitution's Three-Fifths Clause as unfair toward free-labor states. It allowed, he contended, slave-labor states unfairly to enhance their representation in Congress based on their enslaved (nonvoting) populations. He portrayed slavery expansion into the territories as chiefly a threat to "the free institutions of our country." In Belleville in October he charged that Democrats favored "Aristocracy, Despotism and Slavery."[7]

The Republican Party, which had been centrally organized for less than a year, performed well in the 1856 state and national elections. Frémont carried all the free-labor states except California, Illinois, Indiana, New Jersey, and Pennsylvania—the most conservative of these states. Democratic presidential candidate Buchanan carried all the slave-labor states but Maryland, which went to Know-Nothing candidate Millard Fillmore. And Buchanan, by capturing the free-labor states Frémont failed to carry, became president. Nevertheless Republicans won 92 out of 237 seats in the House of Representatives and held 20 out of 66 seats in the Senate.[8]

In Illinois, Republicans, while failing to carry the state for Frémont, elected Bissell to be governor. They performed especially well in the state's northern section, less well in its midsection, and poorly in its south. And Lincoln emerged from the campaign as the state's most prominent Republican. He attributed Frémont's loss to Republican failure to unite with the Know-Nothings, Democratic portrayals of Republicans as favoring "'amalgamation of the white and black races,'" and claims that Frémont was an abolitionist. Lincoln, most other Republican leaders, and a majority of abolitionists looked forward to future success for the new party. A few abolitionists however, influenced by fighting in Kansas, believed the Democratic victory in 1856 required violent direct action against slavery as a strategic alternative to peaceful protest and politics. Among the few were Theodore Parker, Gerrit Smith, and John Brown.[9]

* * *

As he had from the late 1830s through the early 1850s regarding the Whig Party, Lincoln, during the 1856 campaign, tied the Republican Party to the Founders and Henry Clay. The Founders, Lincoln maintained, had deplored slavery's existence and blamed it on the British. Therefore, he suggested, the United States should not foster slavery in its territories. Hoping to appeal to former Whigs, he said that Republicans followed in Washington's, Jefferson's, and Clay's "'old paths'" regarding slavery, which sought to avoid sectional strains. He contended that America's "central idea" was the "'equality of men.'" But he recognized that the nation's "political public opinion" had "always submitted patiently to whatever of inequality that seemed to be as [a] matter of actual necessity." The late slaveholder and compromiser Henry Clay remained Lincoln's "beau ideal of a statesman."[10]

Therefore, unlike such Radical Republicans as Sumner, Seward, and Giddings, Lincoln continued to avoid direct communication with nationally prominent abolitionists. This did not prevent him from expressing some views compatible with those of abolitionists. He sometimes linked the Founders to "the practical equality of men" and to the idea that slavery is morally wrong. At a Republican banquet held in Chicago following the election, he charged Democrats with holding "the opposite idea that slavery is right, in the abstract, the workings of which, as a central idea, may be the perpetuity of human slavery, and its extension to all countries and colors." That same month he wrote privately on behalf of elevating "the oppressed of my species." And, although he continued to share the conventional racism of his time, he diverged from his earlier disinclination to help free African Americans threatened with enslavement. In early 1857 he joined Herndon in assisting a free black man from Springfield who faced enslavement in New Orleans.[11]

* * *

During the rest of 1857 two developments clarified Lincoln's differences from and agreements with the abolitionists. First in March the U.S. Supreme Court in *Dred Scott v. Sanford* decided against black rights and in favor of slavery expansion. Led by proslavery chief justice Roger B. Taney of Maryland, the court ruled by a seven-to-two vote that African Americans were not U.S. citizens. And, in an obiter dictum, Taney added that black people "had no rights which the white man was bound to respect." The court also defined slaves as property that could legally be carried into all U.S. territories. When most Republican leaders reacted to the court's ruling, they emphasized slavery's threat to the interests of free white labor in the territories, the court's legitimization of slavery everywhere in the country outside of the free-labor states, and the fear that the court would next legalize slavery in those states. In contrast abolitionists and Radical Republicans emphasized the negative impact of the *Dred Scott* decision on black rights. To a degree, Lincoln demonstrated agreement with the Radical and the abolitionist point of view.[12]

In a speech at Springfield in June, Lincoln noted that black men acted as citizens by voting in five states. Therefore, he said, "colored people" were part of "'the people of the United States.'" He sympathized with African Americans, contending that their condition had declined during the years since the ratification of the Constitution. Like those abolitionists who by the 1850s had come to embrace colonization, he feared African Americans' "ultimate destiny has never appeared so hopeless as in the last three or four years." But, as always reflecting his and most other white northerners' prejudices, Lincoln added, "There is a natural disgust in the minds of nearly all white people, to the idea of an indiscriminate amalgamation of the white and black races." In his view the Declaration of Independence's claim that all men had an equal right to life, liberty, and the pursuit of happiness did not mean that all men "were equal in color, size, intellect, moral development, or social capacity." Stephen A. Douglas and other Democrats, he added, had gained political advantage by appealing to white northerners' "natural" disgust regarding race mixing and accusing Republicans of wanting "to vote, and eat, and sleep, and marry with negroes!"[13]

For far longer than the Republican Party had existed, white abolitionists had faced similar charges. Many of them had, like Lincoln, responded by expressing disdain for interracial sexual relations. Like Lincoln in his Springfield speech, they noted that the great majority of such relations took place on southern plantations between white masters and enslaved black women. But, unlike Lincoln, most abolitionists during the 1850s did not advocate "separation of the races" as a means of avoiding amalgamation and Democratic charges that they favored it. Even the minority of abolitionists, who advocated black colonization during the decade, regarded it not as a means to avoid racial intermixture but as a way to gain human rights for African Americans.[14]

A second development in regard to Lincoln's relationship to abolitionism was more private as William Herndon succeeded in establishing a tenuous long-distance exchange between Lincoln and Theodore Parker. In 1856 Parker had visited Illinois, met with Herndon, and spoken in Springfield. Given Lincoln's and Parker's similar views regarding Anglo-Saxon superiority, they might have enjoyed discussing the issue of amalgamation versus colonization. But Lincoln was out of town at the time, and they never met. Instead Herndon, who had similar racial biases, continued to channel what influence Lincoln and Parker had on each other.[15]

Among northeastern abolitionists, Parker had become one of the more active in engaging Republican leaders. Even as he remained committed to abolishing slavery quickly throughout the country, he converged with Republicans in emphasizing congressional prohibition of slavery in the territories, banning admission of new slave-labor states, and protecting the rights of white northerners. Beyond obscure Herndon, Parker corresponded with Chase, Hale, Seward, Sumner, and Nathaniel P. Banks of Massachusetts, the last of whom identified with the Republicans' conservative wing. Although Parker had hoped the party would nominate Seward, Chase, or Hale for president in 1856, he had supported Frémont. Writing that year as if he *were* a Republican, Parker had advised former Massachusetts congressman Horace Mann, "I take it we can elect Fremont; if so the battle is fought and the worst part of the contest is over."[16]

It was within this context that during 1857 Herndon sent copies of Lincoln's speeches to Parker, who read them. Parker in turn continued to send Herndon copies of his sermons, lectures, and published writings, which Lincoln may have read. In early July Lincoln and Parker exchanged "best wishes" through Herndon, who pledged to keep their indirect ties secret. As earlier, Lincoln did not want to encourage Democratic charges that he was an abolitionist, or influenced by abolitionists. Parker, who understood Lincoln's concerns, went along because, while he hoped to influence Lincoln, he did not want to injure Lincoln's appeal to Illinois voters.[17]

* * *

In October 1855 Herndon had informed Parker that Stephen A. Douglas had begun campaigning early for reelection in 1858, by the Illinois legislature, to the U.S. Senate, where he had served since 1847. Herndon had added that, when Douglas spoke in various parts of Illinois, Republican senator Lyman Trumbull usually responded to him and Lincoln "sometimes" responded. By mid-1857, as Douglas praised Taney's *Dred Scott* decision, Lincoln responded more frequently as he contemplated running against Douglas for the Senate seat.[18]

Lincoln's task became more difficult that December when Douglas broke with President Buchanan in regard to Kansas Territory. Months earlier a bogus convention, elected to large degree by Missourians voting illegally in the territory, had written the Lecompton Constitution. If accepted by Congress this constitution could lead to the admission of Kansas to the Union as a slave-labor state. When Buchanan urged Congress to do so, Douglas denounced the constitution and Buchanan's support of it as violations of popular sovereignty. This fissure led Republican leaders in and (especially) out of Illinois to urge the Illinois Republican Party to support Douglas for another Senate term. Even Herndon admitted he would vote for Douglas in order "to kill a worse thing—slavery."[19]

As these events transpired Lincoln worked to consolidate support for himself in Illinois and worried about the pro-Douglas inclinations of Republican leaders in Washington and the Northeast. He expressed especial concern about Horace Greeley, the editor of the influential *New-York Daily Tribune*, who led in advocating Republican support for Douglas. Many years later, Herndon recalled Lincoln complaining to him about Greeley and telling him, "I wish that someone would put a flea in Greeley's ear, see Trumbull, Sumner, Wilson, Seward, Parker, Garrison, Phillips, and others, and try and turn the currents in the right directions." If Herndon remembered correctly, Lincoln in 1858 believed the three Boston abolitionists

(Parker, Garrison, and Phillips) had influence in the Republican Party. And in March 1858 Herndon visited Washington where he met with Douglas and Trumbull, New York City where he met with Greeley, and Boston where he met with abolitionists. In regard to Boston, Herndon complained that most of those he contacted, including Parker and Phillips, responded coldly. Garrison however welcomed him graciously.[20]

When Herndon returned to Springfield, he reported to Lincoln regarding the views of Garrison, Parker, Phillips, and leading Republicans. He also brought with him a copy of southern abolitionist Hinton Rowen Helper's *Impending Crisis of the South*. Although Lincoln objected to Helper's endorsement of violent means against slavery, he read the book with interest. But Herndon's effort to enlist the Boston abolitionists in an anti-Douglas effort had only partial success. Parker publicly rejected Republican support for Douglas. Garrison's *Liberator* published material critical of Douglas. Phillips remained silent.[21] This was just as well for Lincoln because Douglas and other Democrats continued to charge that fanatical abolitionists backed him.

Resentment of Greeley's and others' interference in the Illinois election led the state's Republican convention, meeting in Springfield on June 16, 1858, unanimously to nominate Lincoln to succeed Douglas in the Senate. Lincoln accepted the nomination that evening in his famous House Divided speech in which he moved beyond advocating nonextension of slavery. At the start of the speech, as he discussed the Kansas-Nebraska Act and the *Dred Scott* decision, he invoked the biblical phrase, "a house divided against itself cannot stand." He followed by stating that the U.S. "government cannot endure permanently half *slave* and half *free*." Instead, he predicted, "Either the *opponents* of slavery, will arrest the further spread of it, and place it where the public mind shall rest in the belief that it is in the course of ultimate extinction; or its *advocates* will push it forward, till it shall become alike lawful in *all* the States . . . *North* as well as *South*."[22]

Other Republicans had earlier used such phrases as *house divided* and *ultimate extinction*. Abolitionists had spoken and written similarly for far longer. In 1835 William Goodell, who at the time edited *The Friend of Man* in Utica, New York, claimed that either slavery or freedom "must prevail." According to Goodell, either "the laborers of the South will become free, or the laborers of the North will lose their freedom." In 1852 Garrisonian Edmund Quincy used the "house divided" phrase to argue that slavery would either be abolished or destroy the Union. In 1854 Frederick Douglass declared, "Liberty and slavery cannot dwell in the United States in peaceful relations. . . . The South must either give up slavery, or the North must give up liberty." That same year Parker, using the "house divided" phrase, predicted that only one of the "hostile" forces of freedom and slavery could survive in the United States.[23]

Yet, during the 1858 campaign, Lincoln denied that he and the Republican Party owed anything to abolitionist influence. The two candidates' speeches in July and their famous debates that began at Ottawa on August 21, featured Douglas's characterizing Lincoln as an abolitionist and Lincoln's denying he was. Douglas charged that Lincoln's views would lead to sectional war and despotism. He repeatedly denounced Lincoln's defense of limited black citizenship in response to the *Dred Scott* decision. White men, Douglas asserted, had created the U.S. Constitution to serve white interests. African Americans were not capable of self-government. Employing accusations long directed at abolitionists, Douglas accused Lincoln of advocating sexual amalgamation "of superior and inferior races." He contended that Lincoln was an abolitionist who had worked in 1854 with "Fred Douglass and Parson Lovejoy" to bring Illinois Whigs "into the Abolition Camp"—meaning the Republican Party. Douglas portrayed Lincoln as sharing "the most ultra abolitionism of Garrison, Phillips, and the negro Douglas[s]." Conversely Douglas denied Lincoln's charge that he and the Democratic Party plotted "to make slavery national."[24]

In response to Douglas's charges Lincoln, to a degree, stood by his recent statements regarding slavery and black rights. In mid-July he declared, "I have always hated slavery, I think as much as any Abolitionist." He asserted that "vast portions" of the American nation regarded slavery "as a vast moral evil." He reiterated his contention that the Declaration of Independence's equal rights passages applied to African Americans and that every man had a right to the "fruits of his labor." But to a greater degree Lincoln backed off from his recent statements and once again emphasized white rights. He joined other Republicans and many abolitionists in rejecting black-white intermarriage. Unlike the majority of abolitionists, he rejected "social and political equality" and endorsed racial separation. He emphasized slavery's threat to white settlement in the territories. He stressed the *Dred Scott* decision's alleged threat to legalize slavery in the northern states rather than its denial of black citizenship. In addition, while Lincoln continued to describe slavery as "a moral, a social and a political wrong," he denied he supported repealing the Fugitive Slave Law. He denied Congress had a right to interfere with the domestic slave trade. He promised he would not support interference with slavery where it existed under state law or in the District of Columbia.[25]

Toward the end of the debates, Lincoln contended that the contest between perpetual slavery and placing it on a "course of ultimate extinction" could go either way. But immediate emancipation, which abolitionists called for, was impossible. The Republican Party, he said, had to be practical in dealing with slavery, and he again denied he had ties to abolitionists. When Douglas accused him of saying such things in southern Illinois but not in northern, Lincoln responded that he had disavowed abolitionism in Lovejoy's presence in Lovejoy's district. Lincoln called that district "the Abolition District of this State *par excellence*."[26]

* * *

When newspapers published Lincoln's exchanges with Douglas during the summer of 1858, they introduced him to an abolitionist audience that reached beyond Illinois and Theodore Parker. As that audience became familiar with Lincoln, its leaders (following their policy) both praised and criticized him. Parker, who along with a few other abolitionist leaders identified with the Republican Party, initially offered praise. When Herndon sent Parker a copy of Lincoln's House Divided speech, Parker commented, "I think I shall congratulate you on his Senatorial dignity next winter." Later Parker informed Herndon that he took "great interest on [*sic*] the contest in your State, and read the speeches, the noble speeches of Mr. Lincoln with enthusiasm." Frederick Douglass, speaking at a black convention meeting in Poughkeepsie, New York, called the House Divided speech "great." He added concerning the speech, "Well and wisely said. One system or the other must prevail. Liberty or Slavery must become the law of the land."[27]

As the campaign progressed, abolitionists either lost interest in Lincoln or became more critical of him. In regard to the loss of interest, when Massachusetts Garrisonian Henry C. Wright traveled to the Northwest to report on the Lincoln-Douglass debates for the *Liberator*, he centered on Douglas. While deploring that Douglas regarded slavery expansion into Kansas Territory as "*a moral right*," he wrote nothing about Lincoln beyond mentioning his name. The *Liberator* published only a few other passing references to Lincoln, two of which came from Kentucky abolitionist William S. Bailey's *Free South* newspaper. In regard to growing criticism, during mid-July the abolitionist-leaning Chicago *Congregational Herald* wrote of Lincoln's remarks on race, "He made color and race the ground of political principles. He forsook principle and planted himself on low prejudice." H. Ford Douglas, a black abolitionist and former slave who lived in Chicago in 1858, later claimed to have met Lincoln and Trumbull during the campaign to ask them to sign a petition requesting the repeal of Illinois' ban on black courtroom testimony against white people. According to H. Ford Douglas, neither man "dared to sign."[28]

Parker too began to criticize Lincoln. During the first debate Stephen Douglas had charged that Lincoln helped compose the state Republican Party platform adopted at Springfield in October 1854. According to Douglas, the platform called for repeal of the Fugitive Slave Law, abolition in the District of Columbia, ending slavery in all territories, and banning the admission of new slave-labor states to the nation. In reality this platform had been adopted by an earlier, more abolitionist-oriented meeting in Aurora, and Lincoln did not help prepare either that platform or the Springfield platform. But, when Lincoln disavowed most of what Douglas claimed he had supported rather than simply stating that he had not contributed to either platform, Parker objected. Lincoln, according to Parker, had reached lower "anti-slavery ground" than Whig senator Daniel Webster had when he supported the Compromise of 1850. "This is not," Parker lectured Herndon, "the way to fight the battle of freedom." Herndon's assurance that Lincoln had spoken cautiously, based on "honest conservatism" did not alleviate Parker's concerns.[29]

Ohio Garrisonian leader Marius R. Robinson reacted much as Parker did to Lincoln's remarks during the first debate. But Robinson did so in print and in more detail. In the longest abolitionist analysis of a Lincoln-Douglas debate, Robinson's low-circulation *Anti-Slavery Bugle* newspaper, published in Salem, Ohio, stressed the similarity of Lincoln's and Douglas's "principles." The two politicians, Robinson wrote, seemed "far more nearly allied than could be desired by the friends of universal freedom." Robinson praised Lincoln for charging that a Democratic plot existed to spread slavery into the northern states as well as the territories. But, according to Robinson, Lincoln (unlike Giddings and Lovejoy) did not differ with Douglas based on "moral principle." Lincoln denied being an abolitionist, he defended slavery where it existed under "State law," and supported the Fugitive Slave Law. He accepted "consigning . . . [African Americans] and their posterity to hopeless slavery." In all, Robinson charged, Lincoln joined Douglas in conspiring "against liberty and justice, and was unworthy to administer a government for honest men or true lovers of liberty."[30]

NATIONAL IMPACT

R epublicans reacted to Lincoln's performance in the 1858 Illinois senatorial campaign in a manner different from abolitionists. The latter group combined some praise with larger amounts of criticism or silence. Many Republicans approved of Lincoln unreservedly. Although Lincoln had lost the election, they began to consider him as a potential presidential candidate for 1860. This encouraged Lincoln to undertake an 1859 speaking tour during which he visited Iowa, Ohio, Wisconsin, New York, Connecticut, Rhode Island, New Hampshire, and Kansas Territory.[1] During this tour Lincoln often appeared awkward, hickish, and ill-kempt. Yet his brilliant phraseology and insights encouraged Republicans to regard him as a moderate opponent of slavery who could represent northern interests and lead their party to victory. That Lincoln had far fewer ties to abolitionists than his chief rivals William H. Seward and Salmon P. Chase helped him. That he appeared to be less conservative than fellow candidate Edward Bates of Missouri helped as well. But even more than Lincoln's rise within the Republican Party, abolitionist John Brown's October 1859 raid on the U.S. arsenal at Harpers Ferry, Virginia, shaped the 1860 national election campaign, its outcome, and its momentous results.

* * *

In his speeches and correspondence during 1859 Lincoln emphasized the slavery issue in a manner that *could* appeal to abolitionists.

He rejected Stephen A. Douglas's popular sovereignty principle as a means of ending North-South disagreement over the existence of slavery in the territories. He rejected conservative efforts to shift Republican emphasis from slavery to such economic issues as internal improvements and advocacy of a protective tariff. He rejected a Republican and Know-Nothing national coalition based simply on opposition to reopening the Atlantic slave trade. While emphasizing that the Republican Party sought only to "prevent . . . the *spread* and *nationalization* of Slavery," he continued to portray slavery itself as "wrong." In speeches at Dayton and Cincinnati, Ohio, he ridiculed southern biblical defenses of slavery. He reasserted the proposition that regardless of race a worker had a right to what he "earns with his hands and by the sweat of his brow."[2]

In other respects Lincoln's expressions of antislavery sentiment during 1859 continued to fall short of abolitionist standards. Unlike most abolitionists and many Radical Republicans, he sought to accommodate racism in the North and proslavery interests in the South. He objected when Republican congressman Israel Washburn Jr. of Maine voted against admitting Oregon to the Union with a constitution that "exclude[d] free negroes." He opposed an Ohio Republican platform that called for repeal of the Fugitive Slave Law of 1850. Although he recognized that the Declaration of Independence's equal rights principles applied to all, he continued to contend that physical differences prevented black and white people from living together in a state of equality. In notes he prepared in late summer or early fall 1859 in response to charges that he and Republicans favored equal rights, Lincoln wrote, "Negro equality! Fudge!! How long . . . shall there continue knaves to vend, and fools to gulp, so low a piece of demagogism as this."[3]

* * *

As Lincoln conducted his speaking tour, John Brown and his interracial band of twenty-two lived in Maryland planning the Harpers Ferry raid. The raid's historical roots lay in increasing northward slave escapes and the abolitionist response to that phenomenon. During the early 1840s, as Gerrit Smith urged northerners to go south to assist the escapees, a few did so. Most of them, including Charles T. Torrey, who helped slaves escape from the Chesapeake, had ties to Smith's radical political abolitionist (RPA) faction. Some, such as Jonathan Walker, a Massachusetts seaman who failed in an attempt to help slaves escape from Florida to the British Bahamas, had both RPA and Garrisonian connections. Such efforts often led to physical confrontation and violence. During the 1850s resistance to the Fugitive Slave Law and to proslavery efforts in Kansas Territory led some abolitionists and Radical Republicans to become involved in that violence.[4]

These developments raised the number of abolitionists who assumed that slavery could not be peacefully abolished. Rumors of slave revolts, and conspiracies to revolt, contributed to the increase. In 1850 Smith had predicted that black northerners would use "death-dealing weapons" to aid slave rebels. As slave unrest increased in the South during the weeks following the 1856 national election, prominent white Garrisonians declared, "We owe it as our duty to ourselves and to humanity to excite every slave to *rebellion* against his master." Black Garrisonian Charles L. Remond added, "If we recommend to the slaves of South Carolina to rise up in rebellion it would work greater things than we imagine."[5]

Within the context of increasingly aggressive abolitionism, Brown had, during the 1840s begun planning to go into the South to help slaves escape. In 1846 he met black advocates of slave resistance Henry Highland Garnet and Jermain Wesley Loguen. He knew about Torrey and Walker. In late 1847 he told Frederick Douglass that slavery could not be peacefully abolished and that he hoped to lead a band of armed men into Virginia, to recruit the "most restless and daring slaves." Brown hoped these slaves would help "large numbers" of other slaves escape to the North. The civil war in Kansas, during which Brown participated brutally on the Free State side, helped shift his objective from promoting slave escape to instigating revolt. And the publicity Brown gained in Kansas allowed him to get financial backing from prominent northeastern abolitionists. Among them were Smith, Theodore Parker, Thomas Wentworth Higginson, and Samuel Gridley Howe. Smith commented publicly a month before the raid, "For insurrections . . . we may look any year, any month, any day. A terrible remedy for a terrible wrong."[6]

* * *

Lincoln was at home, speaking in and about Springfield, when in mid-October 1859 Brown's band captured the undefended U.S. arsenal at Harpers Ferry, located on Virginia's northern border. The band killed four men, took nine prisoners, and confiscated two slaves. Almost immediately local volunteer companies trapped the band. Shortly thereafter a detachment of U.S. Marines, commanded by Robert E. Lee, killed or captured most of the band's members. Within a few weeks, a Virginia court convicted Brown and the other captives of treason against the state, sentencing them to be hanged in December.[7]

In late October pacifist Garrison called the raid "sadly misguided." Nevertheless he described Brown as "well-intentioned" and "deeply religious." Garrison hoped Brown's execution "as a martyr to his sympathy for a suffering race" would inspire "tens of thousands" to become abolitionists. As time passed Garrison became even more positive in his assessment of Brown's violent means. At the time of Brown's execution on December 2, Garrison declared, "Success to every slave insurrection at the South, and every slave country. . . . Whenever there is a contest between the oppressed and the oppressor . . . God knows that my heart must be with the oppressed." He went on to write, "Give me, as a nonresistant, Bunker Hill, and Lexington, and Concord, rather than the cowardice and servility of a Southern slave plantation."[8]

Abolitionists, who had never been pacifists or who had recanted, viewed the Harpers Ferry raid more consistently. Wendell Phillips and Frederick Douglass praised Brown's actions without qualification. Phillips portrayed Brown as a martyr "in God's service," who opposed wicked proslavery laws. According to Phillips, Brown personified "God's order and . . . law moulding [sic] a better future." Douglass, who had refused Brown's request that he participate in the Harpers Ferry raid, referred to Brown as "the noble old hero." Brown, according to Douglass, had established "a true standard of heroic philanthropy" by striking "the first effectual blow" against slavery when "moral considerations have long since been exhausted." Lydia Maria Child and Parker regarded Brown's raid as the beginning of wider physical conflict over slavery that, in Parker's words, would cause a "Fire of Vengeance" among black southerners that only "white men's blood" could quench. Shortly thereafter Parker, who had hoped that travel would alleviate his suffering from tuberculosis, died in Italy.[9]

Lincoln reacted to the raid quite differently than these abolitionists did. Unlike several of them and some Radical Republicans, he had not met Brown, had no foreknowledge of the raid, and disagreed with its objectives. That autumn he had been concentrating on promoting Republican success in state-level elections, and he worried that the raid could negatively impact perceptions of the party's candidates. Like most Republican politicians, he denied Democratic charges that his party had ties to Brown or otherwise encouraged Brown's undertaking. When in early December, during a speech at Elwood, Kansas Territory, Lincoln first publicly referred to Harpers Ferry, he described Brown's raid as wrong. He said it violated "law" and would not help in "the extinction of a great evil." Lincoln thereby contradicted the abolitionist view of the raid's potential impact. Unlike those abolitionists who predicted a violent end to slavery, Lincoln called for peaceful political action. Yet, like abolitionists and Radicals, Lincoln realized that a minority of northerners viewed Brown's actions positively. Like Garrison before him, Lincoln praised Brown for "great courage" and "rare unselfishness." And the increased sectional tension resulting from Brown's raid weakened Lincoln's dedication to peaceful means. In a speech at Leavenworth, he described Brown's execution as a warning to white southerners who threatened to secede from the Union if a Republican were elected president in 1860. "So, if constitutionally we elect a President," he said, "and therefore you undertake to destroy the Union, it will be our duty to deal with you as old John Brown has been dealt with."[10]

Thereafter Lincoln mentioned Brown publicly only to refute continued southern and Democratic charges that he and other Republicans supported or encouraged Brown to undertake violent action against slavery. In January 1860 Stephen A. Douglas, speaking in the U.S. Senate, maintained that the "outrage at Harper's Ferry [w]as the logical, natural consequence of the teachings and doctrines of the Republican party." He named Lincoln and William H. Seward as leading exponents of those doctrines. In May 1860 the *New York Herald* declared Lincoln to be "as rabid an abolitionist as John Brown himself, but without the old man's courage." That November the *St. Louis Democrat* described Lincoln as "an Abolitionist; a fanatic of the John Brown type; the slave to one idea." According to the *Democrat*, Lincoln, in order to abolish slavery, "would override laws, constitutions, and compromises of every kind, nor shrink, if necessary, from overturning the whole fabric of society, like another Robespierre."[11]

Lincoln most carefully refuted such charges during his speech at New York City's Cooper Union in late February 1860. He portrayed the Republican Party as conservative, favoring Jefferson's vision of gradual "emancipation, and deportation." He said the party would let slavery "alone where it is." Brown, therefore, was "no Republican," and Republicans had not encouraged his raid. Nevertheless Lincoln once again warned white southerners that by their words and actions they encouraged more violence. He charged that proslavery advocates who used Brown's raid against Republicans risked forcing antislavery sentiment away from a "peaceful channel" and toward support for abolitionists like Brown.[12]

* * *

As they had in regard to Illinois' 1858 senatorial campaign, abolitionists took little interest in Lincoln's effort to gain the 1860 Republican presidential nomination. In part this was because squabbling among Garrisonians, a revivalist resurgence, the American Missionary Association's efforts to expand its influence in the South, and the RPAs' increased militancy absorbed their time. Abolitionists did cultivate and criticize Republican leaders in order to push them toward immediatism. But they concentrated on Seward, Chase, Charles Sumner, Henry Wilson, John A. Andrew, Joshua R. Giddings, and John P. Hale—not Lincoln.[13]

During the summer of 1859, when Lincoln had delivered speech after speech, the *Liberator* mentioned him only once and briefly in a column centered on Stephen A. Douglas. Between January 1, 1860, and the convening of the Republican national convention the following May, the *Liberator* did not mention Lincoln at all. This was the case even though some Republican-leaning Garrisonians had lost faith in Lincoln's rival Seward. During the same period, Lincoln did not correspond with a single abolitionist. In late February 1860, when he met Kentucky abolitionist *and* Republican Cassius Marcellus Clay onboard a railroad car in New Haven, Connecticut, he emphasized to Clay the difficulties involved in seeking to end slavery.[14]

On April 23, 1860, the Democratic Party held its national convention in Charleston, South Carolina. There it broke apart over the issue of slavery in the territories. The result was that on June 23, 1860, Northern Democrats nominated Stephen A. Douglas on a platform endorsing popular sovereignty. On the same day Southern Democrats nominated John C. Breckinridge on a platform favoring federal government protection for slavery in the territories. Meanwhile conservative former Whigs and Know-Nothings concentrated in the Border South nominated John Bell on a platform that ignored the slavery issue. The Democratic split, in particular, greatly enhanced Republican chances for victory in the election. Therefore, when that party held its national convention in Chicago during mid-May, those attending sought to nominate a presidential candidate and adopt a platform that would best take advantage of the opportunity.

At the Republican convention delegates could choose among a half dozen candidates. The real contest, however, pitted Lincoln, whose Cooper Union speech had dazzled Republican leaders, against Seward, who had been the early favorite. Lincoln emerged as the winner on the third ballot in part because his operatives in Chicago acted more adroitly than Seward's. More important many delegates, especially those from the Lower North, believed Democrats could more easily link Seward to Brown and other abolitionists than they could Lincoln. Lincoln's supporters emphasized his moderation and his views on issues not directly related to slavery. He had strength among nativists as well as German Americans. People valued his reputation for honesty at a time of widespread political corruption. He supported a protective tariff, internal improvements, and free homesteads in the territories.[15]

To go along with their moderate presidential nominee, the Republicans adopted a moderate platform. It placed opposition to slavery expansion among planks favoring immigrant rights, a protective tariff, U.S. government support for building a transcontinental railroad, free homesteads, and ending government corruption. Beyond slavery expansion, the platform addressed sectional issues by opposing popular sovereignty, opposing reopening the Atlantic slave trade, and opposing the Lecompton Constitution. The platform favored admitting Kansas to the Union as a free-labor state. It ignored *Dred Scott*, the Fugitive Slave Law, and slavery in the District of Columbia. It did not specifically endorse the Wilmot Proviso and, unlike the 1856 Republican national platform, it did not initially include an endorsement of the Declaration of Independence's equal rights principles. A walkout by Giddings forced restoration of the endorsement.[16]

As had been the case in 1856 abolitionists had no direct role in either shaping the Republican platform or in choosing its presidential nominee. And, while abolitionists remained in contact with Radical Republicans, they did not (with the exception of Cassius M. Clay) correspond with Lincoln during the 1860 campaign.[17] Lincoln's nomination nevertheless intensified Democratic charges, North and South, that he was an abolitionist.

* * *

Arch-southern-disunionist Edmund Ruffin of Virginia led among those who leveled such charges. Ruffin had hoped the Republicans would choose a Radical as their presidential candidate because he believed that would encourage southern states to declare independence. When instead the party chose moderate Lincoln, Ruffin nevertheless continued to refer to it as the "abolition" party. The *Charleston (S.C.) Mercury* went further, claiming that the Republicans had rejected Seward because "he was disposed to temporize with the South." The *Mercury* stated that, in contrast, Lincoln, whom the newspaper described as "a fanatic in philosophy, and a vulgar mobocrat," would not hesitate to confront southern "resistance." Northern Democrats joined in characterizing Lincoln as "an extreme abolitionist of the revolutionary type." The *Daily Illinois State Register* contended that "abolitionism . . . has been his ruling idea, the chief article of his political creed, throughout his political career." It claimed that Lincoln was "as much an abolitionist as are Garrison, Gerrit Smith, or Wendell Phillips."[18]

Simultaneously Lincoln's nomination led northeastern abolitionist leaders for the first time to focus extended attention on him. Prominent Garrisonians, including Wendell Phillips, Garrison, and Oliver Johnson, viewed him in a manner nearly opposite to that of southern leaders and Northern Democrats. Shortly after the Republican nomination, Phillips, who had preferred Seward, publicly asked concerning Lincoln, "Who is this huckster in politics? Who is this county court advocate? Who is this who does not know whether he has got any opinions?" Most famously Phillips called Lincoln "the Slavehound of Illinois," based on Lincoln's 1849 suggestion that Congress pass a fugitive slave law for the District of Columbia in conjunction with gradually abolishing slavery there. Garrison, who continued to call on abolitionists to endorse no political party, warned that, once in office, Lincoln "will do nothing to offend the South." For his part Johnson opposed voting for any candidate who did not favor expunging all support for slavery from the U.S. Constitution. All three of these Garrisonians hoped that defeat in 1860 would push Republicans toward immediatism.[19]

More radical Garrisonians, including Stephen S. Foster, Parker Pillsbury, and members of the Ohio-centered Western Anti-Slavery Society went further in portraying Lincoln as proslavery. Foster charged that as president Lincoln would be "a slave-driver general." Pillsbury asserted that "in voting for Abraham Lincoln, you as effectively vote for slavery as you would in voting for Stephen A. Douglas." The Western society compared Lincoln to John C. Calhoun, slavery's late arch-defender, and Daniel Webster, the late arch-compromiser. The society described Lincoln as the "most 'dangerous obstacle' to the antislavery movement."[20]

The most resolute of the RPAs reacted similarly to Lincoln's nomination. William Goodell in early June 1860 declared that he would have "a less elevated conception of . . . [the] intelligence" of "any abolitionist or free-soiler" who voted for Lincoln. A few weeks later, an RPA who worked with free African Americans at Oswego, New York, echoed Phillips by hoping that few men in the town would "vote for a Slave Catcher for President." When, on August 29, the Radical Abolition Party nominated Smith for president, it resolved that no abolitionist should "vote for a candidate like Abraham Lincoln." It pointed out that Lincoln stood "ready to execute the accursed Fugitive Slave Law, to suppress insurrections among slaves, to admit new slave States, and support the ostracism, socially and politically, of the black man of the North."[21]

Some prominent Garrisonians, RPAs, and independent abolitionists, however, applied to the Lincoln campaign their long-term policy of mixing criticism of antislavery politicians with encouragement. In June Frederick Douglass and Gerrit Smith, who each vowed not to vote for Lincoln, praised him. Douglass described Lincoln as "a man of unblemished private character . . . and one of the most frank, honest men in political life." Douglass said that, while "the Republican Party [was] far from an abolition party," it represented "the anti-slavery sentiment of the North." It thereby contrasted with "the wickedly aggressive proslavery" Democratic Party. Even when Douglass endorsed Smith's presidential candidacy and rejected abolitionist support for the Republican Party, he asserted that "great good will have been gained to the cause of the slave by its elevation to power." Smith went further. He expressed confidence that Lincoln was "in his heart an abolitionist." Smith predicted correctly that the white South would react to Lincoln's election to the presidency as if he *were* an abolitionist.[22]

As the campaign progressed several other abolitionists became more supportive of the Republican Party, if not Lincoln. At a Garrisonian Independence Day gathering at Framingham, Massachusetts, H. Ford Douglas had declared, "I know Abraham Lincoln, and I know something about his anti-slavery." It was not so "uncompromising, honest, nor so radical as [that of] you Garrisonians." According to Douglas, Lincoln was "simply a Henry Clay Whig," who shared Clay's view that "'two hundred years of legislation have sanctioned and sanctified property in slaves.'" Douglas went so far as to hope Stephen A. Douglas would win the 1860 election. But in late September

H. Ford Douglas contended that, although there was "no essential difference between the two" candidates, the Republican Party had "a strong anti-slavery element," which would soon bring forth a new party "true to freedom, and . . . the rights of all men."[23]

That same September, Garrison, while still objecting to Republican loyalty to the proslavery U.S. Constitution, contended that a Republican victory in the presidential election would "do no slight service to the cause of freedom." He declared therefore that the Lincoln campaign "has our sympathies and best wishes against its three . . . proslavery rivals." A few weeks later Oliver Johnson, following state-level Republican victories in Pennsylvania, Ohio, and Indiana, wrote privately, "Let Stephen Foster and his sympathizers say what they will, to me it seems utterly preposterous to deny that Lincoln's election will indicate growth in the right direction."[24]

Some abolitionists became even more favorable to Lincoln. Garrisonian journalist Sydney Howard Gay of the *New-York Daily Tribune* and the much younger Theodore Tilton of the New York *Independent*, politically conservative Garrisonian David Lee Child, and Virginia-born nonresistant Unitarian minister Moncure Conway all campaigned for Lincoln. Conway had met Lincoln in Cincinnati during September 1859 and Lincoln's description of slavery "as a moral wrong" pleased him. In July 1860 Conway wrote that if Lincoln and the Republicans won the election "the whole *animus* of the country would be for freedom." Unlike many abolitionists, Conway believed Lincoln stood for "the moral equality of black people." When Conway voted for Lincoln that fall, it may have been the only time he voted in his life. Kentucky abolitionists John G. Fee and William S. Bailey, who had RPA ties, also campaigned for Lincoln. Fee spoke on Lincoln's behalf in Ohio because a proslavery mob had driven him from his Berea, Kentucky, home after he expressed admiration for John Brown. Bailey suffered a mob attack on his *Free South* newspaper office and, like Fee, went into exile.[25]

Among church-oriented and independent abolitionists who supported Lincoln in 1860 were Henry B. Stanton, Elizur Wright Jr., William H. Burleigh, and John Jay. Stanton, a former evangelical, had become a Democrat during the 1850s. Wright, also a former evangelical, had become politically flexible. Burleigh had supported the American Anti-Slavery Society during the 1830s and Liberty Party during the 1840s. Jay was the son of RPA leader William Jay. Second-generation immediatists George L. Stearns and Richard J. Hinton, both of whom had backed Brown's raid, supported Lincoln in 1860. John G. Whittier expressed most directly a willingness to vote for candidates who were not abolitionists. As Lincoln's election became more likely, Whittier informed Chase, "For the first time in my life, I shall vote, I suppose for a successful candidate for the Presidency."[26]

When Lincoln won the election, abolitionists generally reacted with a combination of exhilaration and caution. Whittier balanced his naïve claim that Lincoln's victory amounted to "the triumph of our principles" with recognition that abolitionists had to remain politically engaged for that to happen. Frederick Douglass believed Lincoln's election broke the Slave Power's rule by demonstrating "the possibility of electing, if not an Abolitionist, at least an *anti-slavery* reputation to the Presidency of the United States." Douglass predicted that as a result attempts to revive the external slave trade would end and enforcement of the Fugitive Slave Law would decline. Douglass worried, however, that Lincoln's election would discourage "more thoroughgoing abolitionism." Wright conceded that "honest Abe and his party are thoroughly chained up against everything aggressive and practical." But Wright predicted that Lincoln, even without continued abolitionist pressure, would move toward emancipation. According to Wright, slaveholders would "strike the first blow" in a sectional struggle "and thus make the Republican Party as good an Abolition party as could be wished." Johnson's *National Anti-Slavery Standard* expected Lincoln to "execute the Fugitive Slave bill . . . and maintain the Constitutional rights of the slaveholders as they are generally received and allowed." The *Standard* nevertheless "rejoiced in Mr. Lincoln's election" because "hatred of slavery" gave Lincoln's party "its vitality."[27]

Unlike many other abolitionists, Phillips did not relent following Lincoln's victory. In a speech delivered at Boston's Tremont Temple a few days after the election, he ridiculed Lincoln's limited view of black rights and "the emptiness of Mr. Lincoln's mind." The real victory in the election, Phillips argued, had not been won by Lincoln, who was "not an Abolitionist, hardly an antislavery man." Lincoln, according to Phillips, was only "a pawn on the political chessboard." The real victory, he said, had gone to the "antislavery idea," championed by Garrison and especially Brown. In regard to Brown, Phillips said, "They slew the martyr-chief on the banks of the Potomac; we buried his dust beneath the snows of North Elba." Then Brown's "dead hands" lifted Lincoln to the presidency.[28]

Phillips often allowed his rhetoric to get the better of him, and Republicans portrayed him as a crank. But, just as Wright correctly predicted the Lower South's reaction to Lincoln's election, Phillips anticipated later evaluations of Brown's political impact. As a number of historians point out, Brown's raid advanced Lincoln's prospects. Michael Burlingame writes that the raid helped Lincoln, "who seemed acceptably moderate," defeat Seward, who seemed too radical, for the Republican presidential nomination. Richard Sewell and Hans L. Trefousse point out that Brown's raid ended what chance existed for a Republican coalition with former Know-Nothings and southern Whigs, which would have resulted in nominating a more conservative candidate than Lincoln. David S. Reynolds indicates that Brown's raid contributed to southern demands for additional protection against northern aggression. These demands are what split the Democratic Party along sectional lines, insuring Lincoln's victory. Finally Henry Mayer notes that the bulk of northern voters who sympathized with Brown voted for Lincoln in the general election.[29]

CONTENTIOUS RELATIONSHIP

A braham Lincoln's election to the presidency in November 1860, the secession crisis that followed, his inauguration in March 1861, and the start of the Civil War that April profoundly impacted American abolitionism. These events also led to the first lasting reciprocal relationship between Lincoln and the movement's leaders. Although fractious and sporadic, this was the only such relationship abolitionists ever had with a sitting U.S. president. It existed despite *and because of* Lincoln's and the abolitionists' continued differences regarding slavery and race. Lincoln and the abolitionists also had divergent perspectives regarding secession and war. Lincoln prioritized war to restore the Union. Abolitionists prioritized emancipation. Therefore the relationship centered on abolitionist efforts to push Lincoln toward their goal and Lincoln's sometimes strained willingness to listen to them.

* * *

Following his nomination for the presidency, Lincoln had adopted a policy of public silence. He maintained that policy as president-elect even as the Lower South states left the Union between December 1860 and February 1861. In mid-December 1860, however, he broke his silence to warn secessionists, through the *Illinois Daily State Journal*, that their actions would lead to war, an end to enforcement of the Fugitive Slave Law, increased slave escapes, slave rebellion, and emancipation. Meanwhile Lincoln's friend William Herndon privately assured abolitionists that Lincoln stood "firm as a rock" against compromise proposals in Congress that would permit slavery expansion in return for reunion. Garrison, continuing the supportive policy he had adopted during the election campaign, commented, "It is much to the credit of Mr. Lincoln, that he gives no countenance to any of the compromises that have yet been proposed."[1]

But, for good reason, other Garrisonians and radical political abolitionists (RPAs) interpreted Lincoln's slowness to break his silence as an indication that he would not go beyond opposing slavery expansion to act against slavery in the southern states. Over a month before South Carolina led the Lower South out of the Union, Lincoln had promised to take no aggressive action against slavery where it existed. He stated privately that during his presidential administration "each and all States will be left in as complete control of their own affairs respectively, and at as perfect liberty to choose, and employ, their own means of protecting property . . . within their respective limits, as they have ever been under any administration." In a letter to *New York Times* publisher Henry J. Raymond, Lincoln denied he shared abolitionist or Radical Republican goals. Writing in the third person, he declared, "Mr. Lincoln is not pledged to the ultimate extinctinction [*sic*] of slavery; does not hold the black man to be the equal of the white unqualifiedly." Lincoln assured secession advocate Alexander H. Stephens of Georgia that as president he would not interfere with slavery in the southern states. In early February 1861 Lincoln advised secretary of state designee (and advocate of sectional reconciliation) William H. Seward that, while he "inflexibly" opposed slavery expansion, he did not care about its existence in the District of Columbia and New Mexico Territory or about the continuation of the interstate slave trade.[2]

In contrast to Lincoln during the secession winter, abolitionist leaders preferred disunion and war to proslavery compromise. Gerrit Smith advised secretary of the treasury designee Salmon P. Chase that he regarded breaking the Union as "infinitely better" than "concessions to Slavery." Despite Smith's long-held belief that the U.S. government had a right to abolish slavery, he now agreed with Garrisonians that disunion would promote emancipation. Wendell Phillips expressed his beliefs more explicitly. At Boston's Music Hall, he presented the common abolitionist contention that northern support kept slavery in existence in the South. "Disunion," he asserted, meant "abolition" through slave "insurrection."[3]

Lincoln's inaugural address delivered on March 4 confirmed many abolitionists' fear that he would compromise with proslavery leaders to prevent further secession, slave revolt, and emancipation. In the address Lincoln denied states had a right to leave the Union, vowed to enforce U.S. laws "in all the States," to "reclaim, hold, occupy, and possess" U.S. property in the South, and to "collect the duties on imports." But once again he pledged that he had "no purpose, directly or indirectly, to interfere with the institution of slavery in the States where it exists." He also promised to enforce the Fugitive Slave Law, with the stipulation "that a free man be not . . . surrendered as a slave." The *National Anti-Slavery Standard* interpreted these statements as Lincoln turning "toward the South . . . with both knees bowed down." Lydia Maria Child agreed that Lincoln had "bowed down to the Slave Power to an *unnecessary* degree." Frederick Douglass despaired "for the cause of" the slave under Lincoln's pledge to "prohibit the Federal Government . . . from interfering for their deliverance" and "to catch them if they run away."[4]

As a consequence of the inaugural address, Garrison in a lengthy *Liberator* editorial retreated from his earlier characterization of Lincoln's and the Republican Party's policies as steps toward universal emancipation. He praised Lincoln's "manly courage" in the face of an assassination threat, "rare self-possession and equanimity," and clarity of expression. He asserted that with Lincoln's election "the spirit of freedom ha[d] at last triumphed" in regard to the expansion of slavery into U.S. territories. But Garrison also noted Lincoln's loyalty to the proslavery U.S. Constitution (which also did not protect black rights), Lincoln's opposition to emancipation in the District of Columbia, and Lincoln's vow to enforce the Fugitive Slave Law. Lincoln, according to Garrison, had "no bowels of mercy . . . for those who are seeking their liberty by flight." The new president's attempt peacefully to hold the South in the Union, Garrison predicted, would end either in Lincoln backing down or in war. Like

Smith and Phillips, Garrison at this point preferred that there be no North-South war, that the "covenant with death" be broken, the South become independent, and slave revolt bring freedom.[5]

* * *

When Lincoln's policy of holding U.S. property in the South led to the Confederate April 12, 1861, attack on Fort Sumter and war, both Lincoln and the abolitionists faced difficulties. Lincoln had responsibilities as commander in chief of Union military forces, head of the national government, and leader of a political party. Therefore his challenges exceeded those of any abolitionist or group of abolitionists. During the days and weeks after Sumter, he believed he had to secure Washington, D.C., against Confederate attack, formulate a military strategy to put down what he regarded as rebellion, and convince the border slave states to remain in the Union. He also had to accommodate northern public opinion that demanded immediate aggressive military action.[6]

None of these tasks required Lincoln to alter his long-held views on slavery's legal legitimacy. When he called on loyal-state governors to raise troops, he again pledged "to avoid any destruction of, or interference with property." He allowed Union soldiers to return fugitive slaves to their masters. Fearful that an emancipation policy would drive border slave-labor states into the Confederacy, in a Fourth of July message to a special session of Congress, he emphasized that the soldiers fought on behalf of perpetual union and popular government—not emancipation. In early August he only reluctantly signed Congress's First Confiscation Act, providing for freeing slaves employed by Confederate armies.[7]

These words and actions disturbed abolitionists, most of whom had, as the war began, assumed that Union war aims would inevitably include general emancipation. This assumption had led nearly all Garrisonians to give up disunionism. Most Garrisonians, along with some Quaker abolitionists and some other church-oriented abolitionists, also redefined their pacifism so as to justify fighting a war for general emancipation. Shortly after the Sumter attack Garrison suggested to Oliver Johnson, "It is for the abolitionists to 'stand still, and see the salvation of God,' rather than attempt to add anything to the general commotion." Garrison added, "It is no time for minute criticism of *Lincoln*, Republicanism, or even the other parties, now that they are fusing for a death-grapple with the Southern slave oligarchy; for they are instruments in the hands of God to carry forward . . . the great object of emancipation."[8]

Wendell Phillips, who had been much more critical of Lincoln than had Garrison, expressed similar views in a Boston Music Hall speech. He went so far as to claim, "I have always believed in the sincerity of Abraham Lincoln." To "prolonged cheering," Phillips declared Lincoln to be "right" in his defense of "the Constitution and laws of the United States." Phillips, while noting that he had been a disunionist, declared that "no administration that is not a traitor can acknowledge secession until we are hopelessly beaten in a fair fight." Predicting that the war would end either in "Emancipation or Disunion," Phillips declared abolitionism to be "merged" with American citizenship. Edmund Quincy, who served as associate editor of the *Anti-Slavery Standard*, had declared at the Garrisionian Fourth of July Framingham gathering that Republicans "whether willingly or unwillingly [were] doing the work of Abolitionists."[9]

The previous May RPA William Goodell had called the war a "Second American Revolution," which must end in "a National Abolition of Slavery." Between May and July, Goodell's fellow RPAs Elizur Wright Jr., John Jay, and Frederick Douglass emphasized the centrality of slavery in the war. Increasingly other abolitionists joined in contending that to defeat the Confederacy the Union had to make emancipation its chief war goal. They revived an argument John Quincy Adams presented during the 1830s that the U.S. government, under its war power, had authority to abolish slavery. As the war encouraged antislavery sentiment in the North, surging abolitionist popularity, following decades of abuse and a revival of mob attacks during secession winter, increased their optimism regarding Lincoln. Goodell wrote, "Never has there been a time when Abolitionists were so much respected and as high in favor with the community as at present. Never has there been a time in which their strongest and most radical utterances . . . were as readily received by the people."[10]

From the start of the war, however, a minority of abolitionist leaders continued to express doubts about Lincoln's character. In May several abolitionists objected to Garrison's call on them to forbear criticism of the president's conduct of the war. Church-oriented abolitionist George W. Bassett of Indiana declared, "It is not a war for Negro Liberty, but for national despotism. It is . . . a *pro-slavery* war." At the same Fourth of July celebration in Framingham where Quincy spoke, Stephen S. Foster unsuccessfully offered a resolution opposing support for Lincoln's administration until it fought for emancipation. Frederick Douglass wrote in regard to Lincoln's Fourth of July message, "Any one reading that document, with no previous knowledge of the United States, would never dream from anything there written that we have a slaveholding war waged upon the government." Lydia Maria Child wrote, "Every instance of sending back poor fugitive slaves has cut into my heart like the stab of a bowie-knife." Most negative of all, Parker Pillsbury, speaking at Abingdon, Massachusetts, on August 1, "doubted that Abraham Lincoln would rather abolish slavery than see it continue." Pillsbury declared, "I have no higher opinion of Abraham Lincoln, and his Cabinet . . . than I have of the President and Cabinet . . . of the Confederate States."[11]

* * *

Events, beginning with the humiliating Union defeat in the Battle of Bull Run, fought on July 21 at Manassas Junction just south of Washington, led to more abolitionist questioning of Lincoln's ability, resolve, and intentions. Abolitionists believed the Bull Run defeat increased northern support for their contention that the Union had to fight for emancipation if it wanted to win the war.[12] Because Lincoln failed to share this point of view, and because he continued to accommodate proslavery sentiment especially in regard to the border slave states, abolitionists intensified criticism of him.

Union general John C. Frémont's August 30 proclamation freeing slaves owned by Missourians who supported the Confederacy had a major role in this intensification. Abolitionists had been delighted by Frémont's action. In a public letter addressed to Lincoln, Gerrit Smith characterized it as "the first unqualifiedly and purely right one in regard to our colored population." Smith then proposed recruitment of black men into Union armies. Moncure Conway contended that "when the war is up to the standard of John C. Fremont, the country will be saved." Therefore abolitionists reacted negatively when Lincoln ordered Frémont to restrict his proclamation to slaves used in support of Confederate troops and subsequently removed Frémont from command. Even those abolitionists who had previously restrained themselves regarding the president joined in an outpouring of disdain.[13]

In the *Liberator* Garrison referred to Lincoln's countermanding of Frémont's proclamation as "timid, depressing, suicidal." Removing Frémont, Garrison predicted, would depress northern "moral sentiment and popular enthusiasm." Privately Garrison wrote of Lincoln, "If he *is* 6 feet 4 inches high, he is only a dwarf in mind." Conway wrote to Charles Sumner from Cincinnati that Lincoln had inflicted a "burning sense of wrong" on "the hearts of our own people here, as they gradually see that there is no President of the United States—only a President of Kentucky." Frederick Douglass, commenting on Lincoln's rejection of the "liberation and freedom of the slave" in Missouri, denounced the "weakness, imbecility, and absurdity of this policy."[14]

Lincoln's December 3, 1861, annual message further eroded abolitionist estimations of him and their hopes for emancipation. In this message Lincoln again described preserving "the integrity of the Union" as his "primary object." He opposed turning the war into a "remorseless revolutionary struggle." He suggested that the U.S. government colonize slaves freed under the First Confiscation Act "at some place, or places, in a climate congenial to them," so as to provide "additional room for white men" in the United States. Although a few abolitionists, such as Conway and James Redpath, favored limited voluntary African American colonization in Haiti, Gerrit Smith regarded the message as proof that "Pro-Slavery regard for the Constitution in which he was educated" still "bound" Lincoln. Garrison again ridiculed Lincoln's mental ability, worried that border slave state Unionists controlled his priorities, and concluded that Lincoln had "not a drop of anti-slavery blood in his veins."

Lincoln seemed "incapable of uttering a humane or generous sentiment respecting the enslaved millions in our land." Elizabeth Cady Stanton and Lydia Maria Child joined in deriding Lincoln. Stanton wrote to Smith, "I really blushed for my country when I read that message. But all of his messages have been of the most namby-pamby order. He certainly does not dignify the office he fills." Child called Lincoln "narrow-minded, short-sighted, and obstinate." She referred to his "stagnant soul" and "wooden skull."[15]

* * *

In contrast to such negative, condescending, and dismissive abolitionist reactions to Lincoln's revocation of Frémont's proclamation and Lincoln's December 1861 annual message, a few abolitionists had undertaken direct diplomatic efforts to persuade Lincoln to adopt emancipationist policies. When Lincoln was president-elect, moderate political abolitionist Charles Dexter Cleveland had written to him regarding cabinet appointments. He urged Lincoln not to appoint Simon Cameron because of Cameron's lack of "moral integrity." Cleveland then congratulated Lincoln on his appointment of Radical Republican Salmon P. Chase. Shortly after Lincoln took office, an Indiana abolitionist paid to have the *Liberator* delivered to the White House. In June John Jay wrote to Lincoln suggesting that he urge Congress to pass an act declaring slaves belonging to all supporters of the Confederacy to be free. In early October John G. Fee sent Lincoln an emancipation petition from "a congregation" in Middletown, Ohio. Fee informed Lincoln, "I too am a Kentuckian by birth and life. My home is there. I'm in exile."[16]

As it turned out, despite harsh abolitionist criticism of Lincoln during the summer and fall of 1861, such direct contacts between abolitionists and Lincoln resurged in early 1862 and presaged more personal relationships between some of them and the president. Neither Lincoln nor abolitionists initiated this closer relationship. Rather, during late 1861 and early 1862, as an abolitionist-backed petitioning campaign on behalf of emancipation swept the North, Radical Republicans launched a lecture series at the Smithsonian Institution that brought leading abolitionists to Washington.[17]

The lectures, delivered by Radical Republicans such as Horace Greeley, northern literary figures such as Ralph Waldo Emerson, and prominent abolitionists, began in early 1862. On January 10 church-oriented abolitionist George B. Cheever endorsed "immediate military emancipation," black enlistment in Union armies, and a presidential proclamation (based on the war power) declaring slaves "forever FREE." On January 17 Moncure Conway praised Frémont and described universal emancipation as key to ending the war. Cheever retuned on February 14 to call for repeal of the Fugitive Slave Law and emancipation in the District of Columbia. On March 14 and 16 Phillips praised John Brown, Frémont's proclamation, and Toussaint Louverture, who during the 1790s led Haiti's successful slave revolt. Like Cheever, Phillips called on Lincoln to fight the Civil War for emancipation. That same month Gerrit Smith spoke at the Capitol, although he did not participate in the Smithsonian program. Afterward Smith reported to Irish abolitionist Richard D. Webb, "The most radical abolitionist is now applauded by a Washington audience for his most radical utterances."[18]

Although Lincoln attended several of the Smithsonian lectures, his reaction to them did not rise to the level of applause. Nevertheless, because of the lectures, he recognized abolitionists' increasing influence and greeted some of the speakers at the White House. There, for the first time in his life, he conversed with northeastern abolitionist leaders and demonstrated an awareness of their thought. At these meetings abolitionists in nearly all instances acted respectfully and deferentially toward Lincoln, even as they pressed him to act more aggressively toward slavery. Lincoln in turn treated abolitionists politely, although he often suggested that they had a limited and impractical perspective.

Following Conway's lecture Senator Charles Sumner arranged a meeting at the White House among Lincoln, Conway, and Conway's fellow Unitarian minister William Henry Channing of Washington. Conway recalled that Lincoln "received us graciously" and that Lincoln complimented him on his recent book *The Rejected Stone*. But, when Conway pressed Lincoln regarding emancipation, the president responded evasively. Setting a pattern for his later interviews with abolitionists, he said, "Perhaps we may be better able to do something in that direction after a while than we are now." Lincoln added, "I think the country grows in this direction daily, and I am not without hope that something of the desire of you and your friends may be accomplished." In response to another of Conway's questions, Lincoln claimed that Americans would "hail" him as "their deliverer" if the war ended with slavery still in existence but "on the downhill." He went so far as to advise Conway that abolitionists "over-estimate[d]" their influence and that "the great masses of this country care[d] comparatively little about the negro." Nevertheless, as Conway and Channing left, Lincoln added, "We shall need all the anti-slavery feeling in the country, and more; you can go home and try to bring the people to your views."[19]

What Lincoln may have had in mind when he referred to needing "all the anti-slavery feeling" was a plan he had formulated for federally financed gradual emancipation designed to appeal to the border slave states. He read this proposal to second generation immediatist Samuel Gridley Howe, who served on the U.S. Sanitary Commission, before presenting it to Congress on March 6, 1862. While deploring Lincoln's "habit of procrastinating," Howe exclaimed privately, "The President . . . has at last had a change of heart, and has set his face steadily Zionward!" While Garrison and Cheever regarded Lincoln's limited border slave state plan as another indication of his weakness, Conway, staunch Garrisonian Maria Weston Chapman, and Phillips agreed with Howe. Although skeptical about gradualism, they pursued the alternative abolitionist strategy of portraying the plan as a step in the right direction. Echoing Howe, Phillips declared, "If the President has not entered Canaan, he has turned his face Zionward. . . . So we do believe our President's words are the handwriting on the wall."[20]

When in March Phillips came to Washington to speak at the Capitol, Lincoln invited him to come to the White House. There Phillips pressed Lincoln to adopt more radical measures. Phillips suggested that the president remove increasingly conservative Secretary of State Seward and issue an emancipation proclamation. According to Phillips, Lincoln responded by defending his state-level gradual abolition plan as a means of holding the border slave states in the Union, while reiterating his claim that he hated slavery and intended "it should die." Phillips had already begun considering Frémont as an alternative to Lincoln as the 1864 Republican presidential nominee, and he had privately portrayed Lincoln as "of very *slow mind*." Yet Phillips came away from the meeting "rather encouraged." A month later, after all the border slave states had rejected Lincoln's gradual emancipation plan, RPA William Goodell visited the Capitol and Lincoln. During their White House meeting Lincoln responded to Goodell's criticism of his slow progress toward emancipation with a charming display of knowledge about Goodell's writings. As a result Goodell became even more optimistic than Phillips in regard to Lincoln's future course. Upon leaving the White House, Goodell praised Lincoln's "serious thoughtfulness" and his desire to do "what was best for the country."[21]

The overall abolitionist estimation of Lincoln briefly improved again when on April 16 he signed a congressional measure that immediately ended slavery in the District of Columbia. Abolitionists praised this act despite its provisions for compensation to masters and voluntary colonization for former slaves. Once again regarding a partial action as a step forward, Lydia Maria Child declared, "'old Abe' *means* about right," despite his "hide-bound soul." Oliver Johnson, having previously feared "the undue influence of the Border State slaveholders over his mind," now called Lincoln "a resolute and wise man" disposed to move toward universal emancipation. Black abolitionist leader Henry Highland Garnet, speaking at an "Emancipationist Jubilee" in New York City, requested "three cheers for the Union, the President, and old John Brown." Phillips and Parker Pillsbury reacted more warily. Regarding government steps toward universal emancipation, Phillips in May told those attending the American Anti-Slavery Society (AASS) annual meeting, "Abraham Lincoln may not wish it; he cannot prevent it. . . . Abraham Lincoln simply rules; John C. Fremont governs." Pillsbury worried "that any *good* thing in the Government was quite sure to be followed by some extraordinary baseness." Under Garrison's leadership, the AASS meeting passed resolutions urging Lincoln to move more quickly toward general emancipation.[22]

But Lincoln continued to waver. On May 19, under pressure from border slave state politicians, he revoked Union general David Hunter's order freeing slaves in South Carolina, Florida, and Georgia. Garrison lamented, "To-day a wet blanket is thrown upon the flame of popular enthusiasm by President Lincoln's veto. What giving and taking, what blowing hot and blowing cold, we have upon the slavery question!" Like Radical Republicans and some members of Lincoln's administration, Garrison feared that such a "shilly-shallying course" would frustrate "the friends of freedom" and prompt European intervention on behalf of the Confederacy.[23]

Also, during the spring and early summer of 1862, Congress failed to pass a stronger Confiscation Act. It failed to prohibit Union troops from returning fugitive slaves. And, despite the District of Columbia emancipation act, slave-catching continued there. In response to these developments, abolitionists intensified their appeals to Lincoln, Radical Republicans, and the public on behalf of a presidential emancipation proclamation. Phillips called on Sumner to lead Congress in prodding an "*honest*" but "*timid and ignorant* President." On June 20 Oliver Johnson led a delegation of Progressive Friends to meet with Lincoln at the White House to present a memorial (written by Garrison) begging the president to issue such a proclamation. Lincoln dismissed the proposal. "If a decree of emancipation could abolish Slavery," he said, "John Brown would have done the work effectively." Such a decree, Lincoln believed, could not be enforced in the South. In response to Johnson's advice that "the memorialists are solemnly convinced that the abolition of Slavery is indispensable to your success," Lincoln said that God's way to end slavery might be different than theirs.[24]

On July 4 Frederick Douglass added his voice to those criticizing Lincoln for not making universal emancipation a Union war aim. Lincoln, Douglass said, had "blast[ed] the hope and [broken] down the strong heart of the nation." Like other abolitionists who suggested that military victory depended on setting such a goal,

Douglass declared, "We have a right to hold Abraham Lincoln sternly responsible for any disaster or failure attending the suppression of this rebellion." Such criticism continued as Lincoln drafted what became his Preliminary Emancipation Proclamation.[25]

* * *

Abolitionist pressure had a role in Lincoln's decision to submit a draft of this proclamation to his cabinet on July 22, 1862. Abolitionists also had a role in Congress's passage a few days earlier of the Second Confiscation Act, which declared slaves of disloyal masters to be "forever free" once they crossed Union lines. Nevertheless forces beyond abolitionists more profoundly influenced Lincoln, Congress, and the course of events. These forces included slave escapes, Union battlefield defeats, a need for black Union troops, Radical Republicans, the border slave state rejection of Lincoln's gradual emancipation plan, and the necessity of dissuading Britain and France from joining the war on the Confederate side.[26]

In his draft Lincoln proposed to announce on January 1, 1863, that slaves in areas under Confederate control would be "then, thenceforth, and forever . . . free." But, following Seward's advice, he decided to await a Union military victory before issuing the preliminary proclamation so as to appear to act in strength rather than weakness. As a result, during the summer of 1862, Lincoln's intentions remained unclear to abolitionists. On July 30 Sydney Howard Gay, the Garrisonian managing editor of the *New-York Daily Tribune* and a former editor of the *National Anti-Slavery Standard*, sent Lincoln a letter Gay had refused to publish. The letter, Gay informed Lincoln, represented widespread "deep-seated anxiety on the part of the people" regarding his course as president. It repeated the familiar abolitionist charge that "the President hangs back, hesitates, & leaves the country to drift."[27]

Perhaps anticipating a *Tribune* endorsement of such sentiments, Lincoln, in his first such response to an abolitionist's letter, asked Gay to "please come and see me at once." Although reluctant to go to Washington, where he believed a corrupting political climate existed, Gay visited Lincoln on August 10. Like the other abolitionists who had met with Lincoln, Gay argued on behalf of emancipation, and Lincoln once again did not respond clearly. Therefore *Tribune* editor in chief and Radical Republican Horace Greeley published his "Prayer of Twenty Millions" demanding that Lincoln enforce the Second Confiscation Act and give slaves a reason to support the Union war effort. Lincoln again seemed to equivocate. In a published letter to Greeley, he wrote that because he sought primarily to save the Union he would either preserve slavery or abolish slavery to reach that goal.[28]

In between his conversation with Gay and his reply to Greeley, Lincoln met with a delegation of black leaders. During this meeting he urged the delegation to lead an effort to colonize African Americans in Central America with the aid of funds appropriated in the Second Confiscation Act. He noted the great wrong slavery had inflicted on African Americans and asserted that even when free they would not gain "equality with the white race." Blaming the Civil War on black people, as well as slavery, he concluded, "It is better for us both . . . to be separated."[29] When abolitionists, black and white, learned of these words and shortly thereafter read Lincoln's response to Greeley, most of them reacted with exasperation and ridicule.

Black abolitionist Robert Purvis, in a public letter to Republican senator Samuel C. Pomeroy of Kansas, declared, "Sir, this is our country as much as it is yours, and we will not leave it." Frederick Douglass described Lincoln as "a genuine representative of American prejudice and negro hatred and far more concerned for the preservation of slavery, and the favor of the Border States, than for any sentiment of magnanimity or principle of justice and humanity." Garrison described Lincoln's words to the black delegation as "puerile, absurd, illogical, impertinent, [and] untimely." He attributed Lincoln's outlook to his "education (!) with and among 'the white trash' of Kentucky[, which] was most unfortunate for his moral development." In regard to Lincoln's response to Greeley, Wendell Phillips spoke for most abolitionists when he characterized it as "the most disgraceful document that ever came from the head of a free people."[30]

Yet at least two abolitionists perceived degrees of hope in Lincoln's letter to Greeley. Edmund Quincy, in a *National Anti-Slavery*

Standard editorial, speculated that Lincoln's failure "to save the Union without freeing any slave" and Lincoln's "bold idea" that he could "'save the Union by freeing all the slaves'" meant the president might move in the latter direction. "All good men that love their country," Quincy suggested, should encourage the president to do so. Similarly Gay wrote to Lincoln, "Your letter to Mr. Greeley has infused new hope among us at the North who are anxiously awaiting that movement on your part which they believe will end the rebellion by removing its cause." He hoped Lincoln would soon "announce that the destruction of Slavery is the price of our salvation." He added that "all of the North that is really loyal . . . longs to hear that word from you, Sir."[31]

Quincy and Gay were exceptional in their insight, and military events in early September led most abolitionists to continue questioning Lincoln's fitness to be president. As Confederate general Robert E. Lee's Army of Northern Virginia moved north into Maryland and toward Pennsylvania, Garrison described Lincoln as "nothing better than a wet rag" whose ineptness placed "Washington, Harrisburg, Baltimore, and even Philadelphia" in danger. Phillips called Lincoln "a spaniel by nature" because he had not yet issued an emancipation decree.[32] Then the Army of the Potomac stopped Lee's northward advance at the Battle of Antietam near Sharpsburg, Maryland, on September 17. This battlefield success, which met Seward's requirement, rather than abolitionist and Radical Republican pressure, led Lincoln to issue his Preliminary Emancipation Proclamation.

In this decree, presented five days after the battle, Lincoln repeated the warning to the Confederate states that he had made in his draft. Unless they returned to the Union by January 1, 1863, he would, as commander in chief, declare all slaves within their bounds to be "then, thenceforward and forever free." To those Confederate states that *did* return and to the slave labor states that had remained in the Union (or were occupied by Union forces, such as Tennessee and portions of Louisiana and Virginia), Lincoln promised federal aid for gradual emancipation and colonization. Because Confederate states had no inclination to return to the Union, this may have been the point when a Union war for emancipation and large-scale Union deployment of black troops, which abolitionists had long advocated, became inevitable.[33]

But at the time even many of those abolitionists who had earlier given Lincoln the benefit of the doubt in regard to his emancipatory intentions, had become so disillusioned with him that they reacted cautiously. Garrison advised his daughter Fanny, "The President's Proclamation is certainly matter for great rejoicing as far as it goes." In Garrison's view the Proclamation's deficiencies included leaving slavery legal "in all the so-called loyal Slave States," keeping the Fugitive Slave Law in effect, and waiting until January 1 to proclaim "emancipation in the Rebel States." Garrison conceded that Lincoln's proclamation committed the U.S. "government in due time, to the emancipation of more than three quarters of the whole slave population." Nevertheless Garrison preferred "a proclamation distinctly announcing the total abolition of slavery" to Lincoln's "circumlocution and delay." Independent Massachusetts abolitionist James Freeman Clarke added that Lincoln should have endorsed immediate emancipation "on principles of justice and right not on mere war necessity." George B. Cheever and Goodell characterized the Preliminary Proclamation as designed to use bribes and threats to get the seceded states back into the Union rather than to achieve universal emancipation.[34]

Lincoln's annual message on December 1, 1862, produced a more thoroughly negative reaction among abolitionists as they began to worry that he would back away from issuing a final proclamation. In his message Lincoln called on Congress to provide a plan for very gradual, compensated emancipation combined with colonization of former slaves. "I cannot make it better known than it already is," Lincoln wrote, "that I strongly favor colonization," which, by removing black laborers would "increase the demand for, and wages of, white labor." Upon reading this message, Conway declared, "The President seems to be a man of inadequate caliber; . . . he has exhausted himself . . . in taking up the gauntlet the South threw down." Garrison feared Lincoln intended to substitute the 1862 Annual Message plan for the one he outlined in the Preliminary Proclamation. "A man so manifestly without moral vision," Garrison asserted, "so unsettled in his policy, so incompetent to lead, so destitute of hearty abhorrence of slavery cannot be safely relied upon in any emergency." After receiving "discouraging" letters from Gerrit Smith and Charles Sumner, Garrison continued to believe "the Administration has neither pluck nor definite purpose."[35]

Even so it is likely that abolitionist contacts with Lincoln helped keep him from backing away from the Proclamation after Democrats made significant gains in Congress as a result of the 1862 elections. In response to a report from Wendell Phillips concerning a meeting he had with Lincoln shortly after the election, Lydia Maria Child declared, "At last, I really believe 'old Abe' has got his back up. . . . I think we shall now go ahead in earnest; and, having tried everything else without success, we shall at last rely upon principle." Later that November Cheever wrote to Lincoln, respectfully urging him to transform the Proclamation into one for universal immediate emancipation. In late December Cheever, along with Goodell and Nathan Brown of the American Baptist Free Mission Society, traveled to Washington to present Lincoln with a petition from Cheever's New York City Church of the Puritans that made the same appeal.[36] Lincoln did not take the abolitionists advice. But he did issue his final Emancipation Proclamation on January 1, 1863.

* * *

Black and white abolitionists, including Frederick Douglass, Wendell Phillips, William C. Nell, John Greenleaf Whittier, and Anna Dickinson, had on that day gathered at Boston's Tremont Temple, in anticipation of a copy of the Proclamation arriving by telegraph. When it did not arrive when they expected it would, they became despondent. When it did arrive, they cheered. During the days that followed, some abolitionists echoed that cheer. A relieved Garrison called the Proclamation "a great historic event, sublime in its magnitude, momentous and beneficent in its far-reaching consequences." It would, Garrison declared, "be hailed with joy and thanksgiving by the friends of freedom and human brotherhood throughout the world." Robert C. Waterston of the Church Anti-Slavery Society exclaimed, "This is a great Era! A sublime period in History! The Proclamation is grand. The President has done nobly."[37]

As might be expected, other abolitionists mixed praise for the Proclamation with reservations regarding Lincoln's commitment. At Tremont Temple Phillips described the Proclamation as preparing the way for final abolitionist victory and praised the Union's commitment to fight for it. But, in a manner similar to his reaction to Lincoln's election two years earlier, he attributed the Proclamation to popular pressure on Lincoln, rather than to Lincoln himself. In a tactic that became more common among abolitionists over the next three years, Phillips also called for going beyond military emancipation to restructure southern society and pass laws in order to protect black freedom.

Goodell described the Proclamation as "a step in the right direction, so far as it goes" and declared to abolitionists, "Now is the time to agitate *that* question, and demand Freedom for all. . . . Our vigilance and activity are, by no means to be relaxed, but rather increased." Theodore Tilton regretted that Lincoln had not declared all slaves to be free, while expressing optimism that "Providence means to supplement it [the Proclamation] *de facto*, by adding the omitted states in good time." Some were even more critical. The AASS executive committee described Lincoln as "derelict in his duty" because he had exempted parts of the slave-labor states, and parts of the enslaved population, from the Proclamation. Stephen S. Foster lamented in regard to Lincoln, "Where he had not power to give liberty to slaves in fact, he gave them liberty by law. Where he had power to give them liberty in fact, he did not give them liberty by law."[38]

In late January a delegation led by Conway, which included Phillips, George L. Stearns, and Elizur Wright Jr., brought these criticisms to the White House in what became the most confrontational meeting yet between Lincoln and abolitionists. As had earlier such meetings, this one began amicably as Lincoln advised Senator Henry Wilson who had accompanied the delegation that "he knew perfectly well" who the men were and asked them to be seated. In turn Conway and the others addressed Lincoln respectfully before initiating a more pointed exchange. Conway criticized Lincoln for not issuing the Proclamation sooner. Lincoln contended that the northern public had not been ready earlier. Conway then noted that several prominent newspapers had supported Frémont's emancipation order. Phillips questioned whether the Proclamation was "being honestly carried out." Lincoln responded that abolitionists "may have got into a habit of being dissatisfied." Phillips pledged abolitionist support for Lincoln's reelection to the presidency *if* they could be "sure of his commitment" to total emancipation. Lincoln remarked petulantly that he had been "so abused and borne upon" that he no longer cared about reelection. When the delegation pressed Lincoln to appoint antislavery generals and reinstate Frémont, Lincoln refused. He contended that it was more important to have generals who could win battles. Conway's claim that Lincoln risked losing New England's support did not please the president.[39]

Immediately following the meeting the abolitionists who attended expressed admiration *and* doubt regarding Lincoln. Stearns observed, "It is of no use to disparage his ability. . . . We had the best position . . . but the President held his ground against us." Conway later wrote that the delegation had been "impressed by the powerful personality of the man, by his genius and character." Nevertheless Conway left Washington "with a conviction that the President . . . [despite] all his forensic ability and his personal virtues, was not competent to grapple with the tremendous combination of issues before him." Conway feared "the practical success of the Emancipation Proclamation was by no means certain in the hands of its author."[40]

DRAWING CLOSER AS
CRITICISM CONTINUES

Lincoln, during the final two and a half years of the Civil War, faced complicated issues. Military affairs took up much of his time as he sought a winning battlefield strategy and generals who could carry it out. He confronted a growing northern movement, led by proslavery Peace Democrats, called *Copperheads* by abolitionists and Republicans, who advocated a negotiated settlement with the Confederacy. Such a settlement might preserve slavery and re-enslave people freed by the Confiscation Acts and the Emancipation Proclamation. And, as northern victory in the war approached, Lincoln had to formulate a plan for reconstructing the Union that, he believed, had to satisfy white southerners as well as the radical wing of his party. Within this context Lincoln's relationship with abolitionists changed. Ever since the movement's northeastern leaders had become aware of him, they had combined criticism of him with varying degrees of praise. This pattern continued into 1863. But as that year passed, the movement divided. Some leading abolitionist began to stress praising Lincoln over criticizing him—and he reciprocated. Other abolitionist leaders, who drew closer to Radical Republicans, concentrated more on criticizing Lincoln's apparent lack of resolution.

* * *

This process was neither inevitable nor smooth. Throughout 1863 and well into 1864 all abolitionists often expressed doubt regarding

Lincoln's determination to stand by his Emancipation Proclamation. They questioned his commitment to universal emancipation and equal rights for African Americans. Many of them also held Lincoln responsible for Union battlefield defeats at Fredericksburg, Virginia, on December 13, 1862, and at Chancellorsville, Virginia, in early May 1863. These defeats encouraged calls from Peace Democrats for a negotiated peace that would leave slavery in existence.[1] But in early July 1863 victories at Gettysburg, Pennsylvania, and Vicksburg, Mississippi, made such an outcome less likely. At Gettysburg the Union Army of the Potomac stopped Confederate general Robert E. Lee's invasion of Pennsylvania and shattered his Army of Northern Virginia. At Vicksburg Union forces commanded by Ulysses S. Grant, by capturing the city, completed a geographical division of the Confederacy along the Mississippi River.

These crucial Union victories did not alleviate abolitionist doubts about Lincoln's leadership. They did not convince abolitionists that Lincoln would not seek to negotiate a peace settlement with the Confederacy that would leave slavery in existence. Neither did they increase abolitionist confidence that Lincoln could defeat Peace Democrats in the North. In a letter to Lincoln, William Goodell linked the July 13, 1863, New York City antidraft and antiblack riot to Peace-Democratic "desperation" following Gettysburg and increased black enlistment in Union armies. Goodell urged Lincoln to have Union troops occupy the city in order to save "the country" from Confederate control. Lincoln did not reply.[2]

Yet, as 1863 passed, Lincoln seemed to draw closer to abolitionists. He praised black Union troops, some of whom had distinguished themselves in battles at Port Hudson and Milliken's Bend, Louisiana, and Fort Wagner, South Carolina. He also ceased to endorse colonization publicly. He had previously regarded emancipation chiefly as a means of depriving the Confederacy of human resources. Now he began to perceive it to be God's will, which no human negotiations could reverse. He thereby confirmed proslavery advocates' claim that he *was* a fanatical abolitionist.[3]

On July 30 Lincoln issued an order calling for Union retaliation against Confederate enslavement and execution of captured black

soldiers. Shortly thereafter Frederick Douglass, at abolitionist journalist and former John Brown supporter George Stearns's request,
came to Washington to lobby Congress, the War Department, and
Lincoln on behalf of the continued recruitment of such soldiers as
well as equal treatment for them. On August 10 Radical Republican
senator Samuel C. Pomeroy of Kansas escorted Douglass to meet
with Secretary of War Edwin Stanton, who supported equal treatment. After leaving Stanton's office Pomeroy and Douglass met with
Lincoln at the White House. When Douglass arrived, Lincoln went
beyond his usual courteous behavior on meeting abolitionists. As he
rose to shake Douglass's hand, he said, "Mr. Douglass, I know you;
I have read about you, and Mr. Seward has told me about you." As
Douglass recalled later that year, Lincoln's words put him "quite at
ease at once."[4]

Lincoln knew that Douglass had, in a recent New York City
speech, charged him with having a "tardy, hesitant, vacillating policy." When, during their White House meeting, Lincoln denied that
"such a charge can be sustained," Douglass raised the issue of black
troops. Lincoln responded that it took the bravery of such troops to
overcome white northern hatred of the "colored man" and allow his
administration to move forward on the issue of equal treatment. He
also asserted "that slavery would not survive the War."[5] Lincoln's
apparent honesty and sincerity impressed Douglass. Although he
continued to criticize the president, Douglass began a rocky journey
toward joining those abolitionists who had begun to trust him.

Among these were Goodell and Franklin B. Sanborn, editor of
the Boston *Commonwealth* and another former Brown supporter.
Shortly after his meeting with Douglass, Lincoln had published a letter defending the Emancipation Proclamation as a military measure
and "the use of colored troops" as "the heaviest blow yet dealt the
rebellion." He wrote that "the promise of freedom" motivated these
troops "and the promise . . . must be kept." Goodell responded by
declaring this letter to be "quite as favorable to the cause of freedom
as could have been expected." He praised Lincoln's "clearness, di-
rectness, tact, skill, and force." In November Sanborn privately and
insightfully contended that, although Lincoln continued to make

"feeble declarations in favor of gradual Emancipation" rather than immediate, "he is really all that we desire."[6]

* * *

That fall the failure of Peace Democrats to win northern state elections, Lincoln's appointment of Ulysses S. Grant as supreme commander of Union military forces, and Grant's preparations to invade Virginia further encouraged many abolitionists. So did the role of emancipation in the new Union military strategy, initiated during late summer 1863, of *hard war* against Confederate civilians.[7]

Nevertheless abolitionist criticism of Lincoln continued. Theodore Tilton, who edited the abolitionist *Independent* newspaper in New York City, and Wendell Phillips denounced Lincoln's commitment to *gradual* abolition in Missouri. When Lincoln's Gettysburg Address, delivered on November 19, 1863, did not include straightforward references to emancipation, most abolitionists ignored it.[8] And Lincoln's inconsistent responses to direct abolitionist efforts to shape his policies regarding the standing of former slaves (*freedpeople*) in occupied portions of the Confederacy and in the postwar South caused consternation.

In September 1862 abolitionists associated with the Boston Emancipation League had begun lobbying in Washington. They aimed at the establishment of a federal agency devoted to finding employment for former slaves and guaranteeing their equal protection under the law. In 1863 Josephine S. Griffing, a Garrisonian from Ohio who worked in Washington for the National Freedmen's Relief Association, joined in calling for such an agency, which would also provide food and education. In November of that year, Lincoln met with representatives of abolitionist-inspired freedmen's aid societies and encouraged them to prepare a petition on behalf of such an agency that he could submit to Congress with his endorsement.[9]

But shortly thereafter Lincoln's Proclamation of Amnesty and Reconstruction, which he submitted to Congress along with his annual message on December 8, 1863, reduced abolitionist faith in his good intentions for the freedpeople. Aimed at undermining support for the Confederacy among white southerners, the proclamation offered pardons to Confederates who promised future loyalty to the United States. It acknowledged that the Supreme Court might overrule the Emancipation Proclamation. It did not provide for black suffrage. It suggested that so long as former Confederate states recognized the former slaves' "permanent freedom" and provided for black education, racial issues would be left up to these states to decide.[10]

As abolitionists objected to what appeared to them to be backsliding on Lincoln's part, Wendell Phillips continued to be especially critical. He privately accused Lincoln of proposing to leave the "large landed proprietors of the South still to dominate" and make "the negro's freedom a mere sham." Phillips added in a Cooper Union speech that Lincoln had moved toward emancipation only when pushed, placed black freedom in the hands of a proslavery Supreme Court, and made southern-state reentry into the Union too easy. Phillips declared that the United States owed "the negro not merely freedom—it owe[d] him land, and owe[d] him education." Massachusetts Garrisonian Henry C. Wright acted more directly and diplomatically. In a letter to Lincoln he began by writing, "God bless thee, Abraham Lincoln!" Wright then begged Lincoln to provide him with a handwritten repeat of the part of his annual message in which he pledged *not* "to retract or modify the emancipation proclamation; nor . . . return to slavery any person, who is free by the terms of the proclamation, or by any of the acts of Congress." Lincoln immediately complied. By early 1864 other abolitionists had launched a massive petitioning campaign calling on Congress to pass a universal emancipation amendment to the U.S. Constitution. The Senate, under Radical Republican control, did so on April 8.[11]

* * *

In addition to alarming many abolitionists, Lincoln's Proclamation of Amnesty and Reconstruction split his party. Radical Republicans, expressing views similar to Phillips's, began a nine-month struggle to replace Lincoln with Secretary of the Treasury Salmon P. Chase or former Union general John C. Frémont as the 1864 Republican presidential candidate. As Chase's long-standing political ineptness led to his withdrawal in February, Frémont became the Radical favorite.

During the following months abolitionists divided nearly evenly between those led by Phillips who followed the Radicals in support of Frémont, and those led by Garrison who stood by Lincoln. Members of Garrison's group joined Phillips and Radicals in opposing Lincoln's reconstruction plan. But they believed Lincoln had advanced toward abolitionist views and would continue to do so under their prodding. Tilton, for example, believed the president would stand by the Emancipation Proclamation despite his Proclamation of Amnesty and Reconstruction. Tilton interpreted the message as "only a suggestion" that would not prevent the formulation of a "*better* plan" in the future.[12] As a result of the nomination struggle, both the pro-Frémont and pro-Lincoln abolitionist groups attracted more of Lincoln's attention. He increased his interaction with them—especially with the group that supported him. He gave that group's members greater recognition and praise than he had previously.

In January 1864 Lincoln and the Republican presidential nomination had become central issues at the Massachusetts Anti-Slavery Society meeting. During the meeting Phillips conceded that Lincoln believed "the negro in the end shall be free." But Phillips charged that Lincoln went no further and claimed that Lincoln did not regard "the negro as a man." Phillips called for thorough reorganization of southern society based on free labor and racial equality. In response Garrison agreed that Lincoln deserved "criticism for his slowness" and required "spurring on to yet more decisive action." But Garrison went on to defend Lincoln's character. He declared, "In proportion as [Lincoln] has fallen in the estimation of the disloyal portion of the North, he has risen in my own." Garrison also criticized Frémont for not endorsing the Emancipation Proclamation and suggested that the Frémont campaign would help the Peace Democrats. By a narrow margin the meeting supported Phillips's views.[13]

As the split regarding Lincoln continued, other leading abolitionists sided with Phillips. Despite his earlier praise of Lincoln, Goodell in his *Principia* called for replacing him with "a statesman capable of leading, fit to be trusted, and whose deference to the popular sentiment . . . is not too excessive." Lydia Maria Child commented that Lincoln's policies regarding black Union troops filled her "with indignity and shame." She wrote that "God is doing a great work in this nation, but the agents by which He is accomplishing it are so narrow, so cold!" Susan B. Anthony and Elizabeth Cady Stanton joined in favoring Frémont, with Stanton referring to Lincoln as "the golden calf." The most negative comments regarding Lincoln came from George B. Cheever. He wrote privately, "The man is absolutely incapable of the work given him to do, to say nothing of moral dignity and honesty."[14]

During the spring of 1864 such anti-Lincoln views led extreme Garrisonian Stephen S. Foster and abolition journalist James Redpath to join some Radical Republicans and those Democrats who supported the war (*War Democrats*) in calling for a "Radical Democratic Party" mass convention to meet in Cleveland on May 31 and nominate Frémont for president. Phillips, Elizabeth Cady Stanton, Goodell, and Douglass wrote letters in support. Foster, Goodell, and Parker Pillsbury attended, with the latter two serving on the platform committee. The resulting platform supported the emancipation constitutional amendment. It called for "absolute equality before the law" for "all men." And it proposed confiscation of "rebel lands." The platform, however, did not explicitly call for enfranchisement and land for black men. *And* it included a resolution, which appeared to be designed to attract Peace Democrats by defending their freedom of speech and press against prosecution by the Lincoln administration. Frémont's letter accepting the nomination also appealed to Peace Democrats.[15]

Meanwhile the Garrison group of abolitionists forthrightly endorsed Lincoln for a second term as president. In March Garrison, still claiming to be independent of "every party organization," asserted that to defeat "the Copperheads" the Republicans must have "BUT ONE CANDIDATE" for president and "that candidate . . . must be and can be none other than Abraham Lincoln." Despite Lincoln's inconsistency regarding "the rebellion and slavery" and his "incidental errors and blunders," Garrison contended that the Emancipation Proclamation had "at one blow . . . virtually abolish[ed] the whole slave system." In May Garrison listed additional accomplishments during Lincoln's presidency: in April 1862 Congress had abolished slavery in the District of Columbia; in June 1862 Congress had abolished slavery in U.S. territories, and Congress was moving to repeal the Fugitive Slave Law. Garrison also noted black enlistment into Union armies and Congress's recognition of the black republics of Haiti and Liberia.[16]

At the American Anti-Slavery Society meeting in New York City that same May Garrison once again clashed with Phillips (as well as with Foster and Pillsbury) concerning Lincoln. Shortly thereafter Garrison and Tilton decided to attend the Republican (or Union) national convention held in Baltimore on June 7 and 8. Observing the convention from a gallery, Garrison applauded Lincoln's unanimous renomination, antislavery speeches, and a resolution endorsing the universal emancipation amendment. From Baltimore Garrison and Tilton went on to Washington.[17]

On June 9 Tilton and Judge Hugh Lennox Bond, a Baltimore abolitionist, escorted Garrison to the White House, where delegates from the Baltimore convention had come to congratulate Lincoln on his renomination. As he had with Douglass the previous August, Lincoln greeted Garrison "very warmly" and, so that they might speak privately, invited him to return the next day. At that meeting, which lasted an hour, Garrison recalled his criticism of Lincoln during 1861 and 1862. He added that since then Lincoln had earned his "hearty support and confidence" by issuing the Emancipation Proclamation and expressing determination "to stand by it." Lincoln responded "good-naturedly" and revealed that he had suggested the emancipation amendment resolution to the Baltimore convention. He expressed hope that the House of Representatives would join the Senate in passing the amendment.[18]

Lincoln valued Garrison's understanding of the diverse currents of opinion and politics with which he dealt. And Garrison remained supportive even as Lincoln, in early July, pocket vetoed the Wade-Davis Bill, which outlined a slightly more stringent program for restructuring the South than had Lincoln's Proclamation of Amnesty and Reconstruction. By this time Garrison had become more loyal to Lincoln than were Charles Sumner and other Radical Republicans. When Moncure Conway, who had moved to England, questioned

Lincoln's commitment to black citizenship and treatment for black soldiers, Garrison publicly criticized Conway. According to Garrison, Conway had pretentiously assumed that he had moral superiority over "President Lincoln and his administration." Lincoln, Garrison wrote, did not have "a callous heart or a pro-slavery disposition." Though bound by the restraints on his office, Lincoln had taken "long strides . . . in the right direction, and never a backward step" in formulating a "grand and far-reaching anti-slavery measures."[19]

Other leading abolitionists joined Garrison in siding with Lincoln. The president's private secretary John Hay reported, "[James] Miller McKim and other distinguished radical abolitionists are entirely satisfied that the President is . . . 'the wisest radical of them all.'" Tilton advised arch-Lincoln-critic Parker Pillsbury that God had predestined Lincoln's presidency. Oliver Johnson berated Cheever and Goodell for their involvement in a Frémont movement that would help Confederate president Jefferson Davis. Wright, Franklin B. Sanborn, McKim, Tilton, and black abolitionists John Mercer Langston and James W. C. Pennington actively supported Lincoln. So did fluctuating Lydia Maria Child. In mid-August Gerrit Smith, in a public letter to Republican U.S. senators Benjamin F. Wade and Henry Winter Davis, acknowledged that Lincoln had at times "fallen into grave errors." But Smith wondered who, in "his perplexing circumstances would not err." Smith speculated that "the national existence" might depend on Lincoln's reelection.[20]

* * *

The conflicting abolitionist views of Lincoln had several causes. They included diverging concepts of agitation, varying degrees of flexibility regarding how to reach their goals, and differing personalities. The divergent views also reflected rapidly changing circumstances, Lincoln's frequently ambiguous statements, and his reticence. Confusion resulted and Anna Dickinson, a very popular young abolitionist spokeswoman, exemplified it. In January 1864 she had addressed the House of Representatives, with Abraham and Mary Lincoln in attendance. In her speech Dickinson criticized Lincoln's Proclamation of Amnesty and Reconstruction *and* called for his reelection.

During an April visit to the White House, Dickinson told Lincoln that his plan for reconstruction was "all wrong; as radically bad as can be." Despite Tilton's attempt to restrain her, during a speech at Grover's Theater in Washington a month later, she criticized Lincoln and praised Frémont.[21]

Throughout the summer of 1864 many Radical Republicans and some prominent abolitionists continued to advocate Frémont as Lincoln's presidential replacement. Meanwhile Democrats persisted in portraying Lincoln as an abolitionist who, by rejecting negotiations with the Confederacy regarding slavery, prolonged a disastrous war. For his part Lincoln began to doubt he could be reelected, while continuing to vacillate regarding slavery and black rights. He feared that, without his reelection, there would be no universal emancipation. But he also contemplated leaving "our remaining dispute about slavery . . . to the peaceful tribunals of courts and votes."[22]

As he pondered the future Lincoln invited Frederick Douglass to make a second visit to the White House. Douglass's public observations that Lincoln considered black men "good enough to fight for the government, but not good enough to vote" and would thereby "hand the negro back to the political power of his master" prompted Lincoln's invitation. When Douglass arrived at Lincoln's office on August 19 he found the president in an "alarmed condition" due to pressure "for peace at almost any price." The Democratic Party had nominated proslavery former Union general George B. McClellan for president. McClellan's prospects, according to Douglass, appeared to be as "bright" as "Lincoln's were gloomy." Lincoln showed Douglass a draft letter he had "written with a view to meet the peace clamor raised against him." In the letter Lincoln pledged to "not make the abolition of slavery an absolute prior condition to the reestablishment of the Union." Well aware of how Douglass would react, Lincoln asked him, "Shall I send forth this letter?" Douglass replied, "Certainly not. It would be given a broader meaning than you intend to convey; it would be taken as a complete surrender of your anti-slavery policy, and do serious damage."[23] As it turned out, Lincoln followed Douglass's advice.

During the remainder of the two men's conversation Lincoln brought up a more specific version of the issue Douglass had raised

regarding black freedom. Concerned that the fall elections would result in Democratic control of the U.S. government, Lincoln "alarmed"
his guest by expressing fear that only those slaves who "*succeeded
in getting within our lines would be free after the war was over.*" He
asked Douglass to devise a plan to spread news of the Emancipation
Proclamation among slaves and get them to Union lines. Lincoln told
Douglass that he hoped such an undertaking would secure slaves'
freedom *and* weaken the Confederacy. Lincoln's apparent frank-
ness, concern for black freedom, and demeanor once again alleviated
Douglass's doubts about his sincerity. Douglass later said, "He treated
me as a man; he did not let me feel for a moment that there was any
difference in the color of our skins." Lincoln in turn observed that
Douglass had risen from slavery to become "one of the most meritori-
ous men in America."[24]

Within ten days of his meeting with Lincoln, Douglass talked
with "several trustworthy and Patriotic Colored men" regarding how
to provoke slave escapes. Douglass then suggested to Lincoln how
such a plan might be carried out. Two developments made it unnecessary. First the Democratic nomination of McClellan united
Republicans in support of Lincoln. Second the capture of the key
Confederate city of Atlanta on September 1 by a Union army commanded by William Tecumseh Sherman assured Lincoln's reelection.
Abolitionists loyal to Lincoln, including Smith, Howe, and Whittier,
urged Frémont to withdraw, which he did on September 22. A few
days earlier Douglass endorsed Lincoln in a letter to Garrison. In
this letter Douglass declared that "every man who wishes well to the
slave and to the country should at once rally with all the warmth
and earnestness of his nature to the support of Abraham Lincoln."[25]

In early October Smith indicated he had been "spending a great
deal [of money] for the election of Lincoln." Anna Dickinson, although still critical of Lincoln, campaigned for him. She joined
Tilton, Henry C. Wright, Smith, Marius R. Robinson, Theodore
Weld, Ichabod Codding, Calvin Fairbank, Sallie Holley, John A.
Rogers, and black abolitionist Sojourner Truth. Truth, who had been
in Michigan, spoke on Lincoln's behalf several times in New Jersey
as she traveled to Washington to work for the National Freedmen's

Relief Association. In Washington Lucy N. Coleman, a white abolitionist who worked for the National Association for the Relief of Destitute Colored Women and Children, arranged through local black activist (and Mary Lincoln confidant) Elizabeth Keckley for Truth to meet with Lincoln. Truth, like Douglass and Garrison, regarded the Emancipation Proclamation as the turning point toward full black freedom. She greeted Lincoln by praising him as "the best President" and calling him God's "instrument." Lincoln, as usual, responded graciously and humbly. A few weeks later Truth reported, "I was never treated by any one with more kindness and cordiality than was shown to me by that great and good man."[26]

Lincoln's more resolute abolitionist critics still did not agree. In a public letter to Garrison, published the day after Frémont withdrew, George L. Stearns (while denying he was "a partisan of the Frémont movement") described Lincoln as "unfitted by nature and education to carry on the government for the next four years." Shortly thereafter Elizabeth Cady Stanton lamented that "one by one our [abolitionist] giants" had endorsed Lincoln. She exclaimed, "What impudence to ask the people to accept another four years under the same dynasty." Phillips approached irrationality in a speech in Boston on October 20, when he characterized Lincoln as "vigorous, despotic, decisive everywhere else," but "tender . . . towards the South." He accused Lincoln of being "unduly and dangerously reluctant . . . to approach the negro or use his aid." Phillips pledged to "agitate until I bayonet him [Lincoln] and his party into justice."[27]

Yet abolitionists of all persuasions welcomed Lincoln's and the Republican Party's triumph in the November election "as a great victory for freedom." The election result, they believed, would allow them to continue pressing Lincoln and his party for action on behalf of universal emancipation and federal protections for black rights. Phillips portrayed Lincoln's reelection as an opportunity for abolitionists to "rally together to claim of the Republican party the performance of their pledge—amendments to the constitution; that puts [sic] *things* beyond *men* in all time to come."[28]

On December 6 Lincoln issued his annual message, which included a recommendation that the House of Representatives join the Senate in passing the "proposed amendment to the Constitution abolishing slavery throughout the United States." Lincoln also reaffirmed his vow not to modify the Emancipation Proclamation or allow the re-enslavement of anyone freed under it or by an act of Congress. Abolitionist leaders responded by pressing ahead with their effort to make sure both of these things took place, although they remained divided in their approaches. Representing those abolitionists who stressed the positive, Oliver Johnson wrote to Lincoln lauding his "noble words." Johnson interpreted these words as a pledge on Lincoln's part to "exterminate slavery, root and branch, from the American soil." Lincoln, according to Johnson, had "justified the confidence which the great body of Abolitionists, led by Wm. Lloyd Garrison have placed in you."[29]

Representing those abolitionists who emphasized the negative, Phillips accused Lincoln of being too eager to make peace with the Confederacy. Phillips then traveled to Washington to meet with Radical Republican congressmen who believed Lincoln's reconstruction plan would allow southern states to keep African Americans in semi-slavery. Phillips reported to Elizabeth Cady Stanton that the Radicals believed "Lincoln with his immense patronage can do what he pleases; the only hope is an appeal to the people." Stanton in turn advised Susan B. Anthony that because Garrison, Smith, and other prominent abolitionists accepted Lincoln's policies "come what will, then Phillips and a few others must hold up the pillars of the temple."[30]

* * *

During the early months of 1865, as the Civil War and his life neared conclusion, Lincoln drew closer to those abolitionists who supported him. For much of January he and his administration worked behind the scenes with members of the House of Representatives to secure the two-thirds vote necessary to pass what became the Thirteenth Amendment to the U.S. Constitution ending legal slavery throughout the country. The effort succeeded on January 31 with black abolitionist minister Henry Highland Garnet seated in the House gallery. Afterward Lincoln and several Republican congressmen arranged for Garnet to preach in the House in mid-February. On that occasion

Garnet celebrated passage of the amendment. He also pressed for federal government support for black voting rights and education.[31]

Phillips and a bare majority of abolitionists joined Garnet in calling for congressional action on behalf of these objectives. In contrast Garrison had come to believe that ratification of the Thirteenth Amendment providing universal emancipation would culminate the abolitionist movement. In a speech at Boston's Music Hall, he credited Lincoln with opening the way for this achievement. Nevertheless, based on Boston businessman John M. Forbes's observation that Lincoln regarded Garrison as "a radical, with a substratum of common sense and practical wisdom," Garrison hoped to continue to influence Lincoln's actions.[32]

Ten days before the House passed the emancipation amendment, Garrison had written to Lincoln in regard to William Tolman Carlton's painting *Watch Meeting, Dec. 31st, 1862, Waiting for the Hour*, which a group of women had purchased and sent as a gift to Lincoln the previous July. The painting depicts African Americans awaiting news of the Emancipation Proclamation. In his letter to Lincoln, Garrison mentioned that Lincoln had not acknowledged receipt of the painting, although people had seen it in the White House. Garrison went on to point out that since he had met with Lincoln he had defended him in the *Liberator* and in speeches "against the many sweeping accusations that have been brought against you, sometimes even on the anti-slavery platform." Garrison added, "God be with you to the end, to strengthen, enlighten, inspire your mind and heart, and render your administration illustrious to all coming ages!"[33]

Lincoln quickly but briefly acknowledged that he had received the painting and apologized to Garrison for not doing so earlier. Then Garrison on February 13 repeated to Lincoln his wish that God would sustain him "to the end!" As an "instrument in his hands," Garrison declared, Lincoln had "done a mighty work for the freedom of millions who have so long pined in bondage in our land—nay for the freedom of all mankind." Garrison added, "I am sure you will consent to no compromise that will leave a slave in his fetters."[34]

These words suggest Garrison's awareness that Lincoln might still accept compromise with the white South. That same February

Radical Republicans in the U.S. Senate led by Charles Sumner defeated an attempt to readmit Louisiana under Lincoln's mild reconstruction policy that would not protect black rights. Phillips, Elizur Wright Jr., and Douglass praised Sumner and other Radicals. In contrast, when Lincoln learned of the Radicals' action, he complained privately that they had gone too far on behalf of black rights. He contended that those who insisted on giving black men the right to vote as a condition for readmitting a state to the Union, sought "to change this government from its original form and make it a strong centralized power."[35]

Yet when Douglass attended Lincoln's second inauguration on March 4 the two men's friendly relationship continued. In his inaugural address Lincoln portrayed slavery as a national sin that would end with Union victory in the Civil War. He did not address the issue of black rights. But that evening Lincoln demonstrated a willingness to act on behalf of Douglass's rights and an appreciation of Douglass's judgement. When police at the White House door attempted to block Douglass from attending the presidential reception, Lincoln had him escorted into the East Room. As Douglass entered the room, Lincoln exclaimed, "Here comes my friend Douglass." After the two men shook hands, Lincoln mentioned that he had seen Douglass in the crowd as he delivered his address and asked Douglass what he thought of it. Douglass responded, "Mr. Lincoln, it was a sacred effort."[36]

Later Douglass compared the address to "a sermon." He admired its contention that the Civil War constituted God's punishment of both sections of the country for "the bond-man's two hundred and fifty years of unrequited toil." He even praised Lincoln's vow to end the war "with malice toward none and charity for all." In the *Liberator* Garrison also praised Lincoln for contritely recognizing "the chastising hand of Divine Providence for our great national sin of slavery." Garrison added that the address would "inspire fresh confidence in the integrity and firmness of the President touching that hateful system, and deepen the popular feeing as to the duty and necessity of utterly abolishing it in the present struggle."[37]

Lincoln in turn recognized the abolitionists' contribution. Toward the end of March he left Washington to visit Grant at the general's headquarters in City Point, Virginia. After Richmond fell to Union troops on April 3, Lincoln went on to visit that city where black residents greeted him as their liberator. At nearby Petersburg, Lincoln again met with Grant and spoke briefly with Lieutenant Daniel H. Chamberlain, a white officer of the Fifth Massachusetts regiment of black cavalry. Many years later Chamberlain, who served as Republican governor of South Carolina from 1874 to 1876, recalled thanking Lincoln "for his great deliverance of the slaves." According to Chamberlain, Lincoln (who rarely portrayed himself as shaping events) responded, "I have only been an instrument. The logic and moral powers of Garrison, and the anti-slavery people of the country and the army have done all."[38]

Lincoln further recognized the abolitionist role following Lee's surrender at Appomattox on April 9. He did so by suggesting that Secretary of War Stanton invite Garrison, along with Tilton, Joshua Leavitt, George Thompson, and Garrison's son George, who served in the Union army, to join the victory celebration at Fort Sumter on April 14. Therefore Garrison and the others were in South Carolina when they learned that John Wilkes Booth, claiming that Lincoln was an abolitionist similar to John Brown, had assassinated Lincoln in Washington.[39]

* * *

Abolitionist reactions to this tragic event reflected the fraught relationship that had long existed between them and Lincoln. Retrospective disregard and distrust of Lincoln persisted among some. Others became increasingly devoted to positive memories of him. Nearly all mentioned the differences between Lincoln's and their points of view regarding slavery and what they considered to be his deficiencies. All, to varying degrees, recognized his progress toward what they regarded as enlightenment and their growing respect for him. Phillips remained most critical. Lincoln, he said in a speech delivered at Boston's Tremont Temple on April 23, was "unable to lead and form the nation, he was content to be only its representative and mouthpiece." According to Phillips, Lincoln, "with prejudices hanging about him . . . groped his way very slowly and sometimes reluctantly forward." But Phillips also contended that history would judge Lincoln equal to Washington, Hamilton, Franklin, and Jefferson. He praised Lincoln, much as Douglass and Garrison had earlier, as God's instrument.[40]

Lydia Maria Child, in a public letter to Tilton, acknowledged Lincoln's "deficiencies which sorely tried the patience of radicals." She recalled that "after the publication of his first inaugural, I said I would never forgive Abraham Lincoln." Yet she also recalled her growing respect for Lincoln's leadership. She characterized him as "a good and great man." She praised him for "charm in his unsophisticated way of talking with the people when they called on him for a speech" and the profundity of his "grander utterances." Lincoln, she had come to appreciate, had held together "many refractory forces" to achieve "the desired result." She observed that "one rarely sees such honest unselfishness of purpose combined with as much shrewdness in the dealing with men for the accomplishment of purpose.[41]

Both Douglass and Garrison spoke about Lincoln on June 1 at the end of the nation's official period of mourning. At Cooper Union, Douglass, using a phrase similar to the one he used years later at the dedication of the Freedmen's Monument, described Lincoln as "unsurpassed by any in his regard for the white man." But, in contrast to the later speech, Douglass also proclaimed Lincoln to be "emphatically the black man's president." Lincoln, according to Douglass, was the first U.S. president "to show any interest in the rights of the black man, or to acknowledge that he had any rights the white man had to respect."[42]

Garrison, speaking at a Union League meeting in Providence, Rhode Island, provided the most sophisticated postmortem abolitionist account of Lincoln's character and relationship to the movement's goals. Lincoln, Garrison noted, had never "assume[d] to be an abolitionist" and supported the U.S. Constitution as a proslavery document. During the 1850s Lincoln had "participated in the moral blindness and terrible infatuation which . . . prevailed in the country." When the Civil War began Lincoln had defended slaveholders' rights, upheld the Fugitive Slave Law, and "ignored the necessary and palpable relation of slavery to the rebellion." Like Phillips (and to a degree Lincoln himself) Garrison noted that Lincoln had been criticized for lacking "insight or decision . . . timidly following instead of boldly leading public sentiment." But, like Child, Garrison recognized "the appalling difficulties of . . . [Lincoln's] situation." Garrison acknowledged as well that Lincoln was a politician, not "a philanthropist or reformer, in a radical sense."

Garrison placed Lincoln's early political career in proslavery, anti-abolitionist Illinois and in Congress in a most positive perspective. He praised Lincoln for speaking against slavery and in favor of petitioning, abolition in the District of Columbia, and the Wilmot Proviso, despite the fact that Lincoln's positions on all these issues fell short of those of abolitionists. Noting Lincoln's "humble origin," Garrison praised "the vigor and sagacity of his mind," his "unselfish and ever active patriotism," and "his plainness of speech." Again in contrast to Phillips, Garrison described Lincoln as a president who had been "strong and resolute in adhering to the right, as revealed to his understanding." According to Garrison, when Lincoln changed "his position," it "was always a step in advance."[43]

CONCLUSION

By the time of Abraham Lincoln's death, what had begun as a distant relationship between him and abolitionists had grown closer and more personal. Much about Lincoln, the abolition movement, and the United States had changed since the time when abolitionists first impacted his life by encouraging the outlawing of slavery in Illinois. They had thereby helped shape Lincoln's youthful environment and the cultural and economic climate in which he came to maturity. During the 1830s abolitionist actions and concerns led Lincoln, as a fledgling politician, to address issues related to slavery. During the 1840s the abolitionists impacted the course of Lincoln's political career at the national level. Their opposition to the war against Mexico and their demand for emancipation in the District of Columbia especially influenced him during his term in Congress between 1847 and 1849. By the mid-1850s the abolitionists who helped organize the Illinois Republican Party encouraged Lincoln to address the slavery issue more directly.

Yet Lincoln never fully endorsed abolitionist views and goals. Factors beyond abolitionism had a more profound impact on his personality, political orientation, racial views, and outlook regarding slavery. Those factors included his Border South background, life on the northwestern frontier, political ambition, and Whiggish nationalism. Slaveholding politicians Thomas Jefferson and Henry Clay set examples for Lincoln's moderately antislavery and racially prejudiced views during the antebellum decades. A Whig Party tradition of compromise regarding slavery, northern commitment to wage labor, and widespread northern sentiment in favor of preserving western territories for free-white farmers determined the course of Lincoln's political career. All of this contrasted with abolitionists' radical commitment to universal emancipation and black rights.

Unlike a few Radical Republican politicians, Lincoln did not at any time in his life affiliate with an abolitionist organization. Unlike a larger number of Radical and Moderate Republicans, he never attended an abolitionist meeting or shared a podium with an abolitionist. Instead, prior to the Civil War, Lincoln distanced himself from abolitionist leaders such as William Lloyd Garrison, Gerrit Smith, and Frederick Douglass. They in turn took little interest in him.

Even by 1858, as Lincoln cautiously and indirectly sought contacts with northeastern abolitionist leaders, he regarded them as dangerous fanatics. Based on personal experience, he feared Democrats' use of such contacts, real and imagined, to harm his and the Republican Party's electoral prospects. He also believed that abolitionist encouragement of slave escapes, abolitionist-inspired resistance to the Fugitive Slave Law of 1850, and abolitionist threats to slavery in the southern states posed a greater threat to the Union than the dispute over slavery in the territories.

It took Lincoln's emergence as the Republican presidential candidate in 1860, his election to that office, the secession of Lower South states, his inauguration in March 1861, and the beginning of the Civil War a month later to initiate a transformation of his relationship with abolitionists. This process culminated during the final years of the Civil War, his presidency, and his life. Abolitionists, despite differences among themselves, believed secession and war provided an opportunity to destroy slavery and establish equal rights for African Americans. As members of a radical movement for racial justice, they sought to push Lincoln, his administration, Congress, and U.S. armed forces toward action on behalf of these goals. Often Lincoln's apparent racism, devotion to colonizing African Americans outside the United States, and commitment to enforcing the Fugitive Slave Law seemed to stand in the way. So did his evasiveness and expressed willingness to preserve slavery as the price of reunion. But as the course of the war led Lincoln to support antislavery policies as war measures, many abolitionists saw signs of hope.

Garrison led such abolitionists as they became by degrees, and with much trepidation, loyal Lincoln supporters. They came to believe his increasingly aggressive policies toward slavery would lead to the achievement of their long-term objectives. As abolitionists visited Washington to speak and lobby, Lincoln met with them, exchanged views with them, and on occasion charmed them. Even so a large portion of the abolitionists continued to distrust his leadership and intentions.

These tensions within Lincoln's relationship with the abolitionists and within the abolition movement concerning him remained after his death. They are most dramatically evident in Douglass's eulogy for Lincoln in June 1865 and Douglass's more critical evaluation ten years later, summarized in this book's introduction. An understanding of the long-term development of this stressful evolving relationship not only reveals a great deal about Lincoln and the abolitionists. It also provides insight into the complexities involved in northern politics, society, and culture during the Civil War era.

ACKNOWLEDGMENTS

I thank Richard W. Etulian and Sylvia Frank Rodrigue for asking me to write this book for the Concise Lincoln Library series. I also thank them, an anonymous reader, Douglas R. Egerton, and John R. Kaufman-McKivigan for their careful readings of my manuscript. Their insights and suggestions helped make this a better book than it would have been otherwise. So did Amy Alsip's careful copyediting of my manuscript. Heather Furnas of the Samuel J. May Antislavery Collection at Cornell University Library, Tammy Kiter of the New-York Historical Society, and Kimberly Reynolds of Boston Public Library were especially helpful in locating manuscript letters used in this book. I am grateful to the staffs of the Interlibrary Loan, Government Documents, and Microforms Departments at the University of South Carolina for their help. Finally I thank Emily Harrold for her crucial assistance in downloading high-quality images for the photo gallery, and Judy Harrold for her equally crucial technical assistance.

NOTES

Introduction

1. Douglass, "Oration."
2. Douglass, "Oration."

1. Different Worlds

1. Locke, *Anti-Slavery*, 97–99, 101–11. See also Newman, *Transformation of American Abolitionism*, 4–20.
2. Gienapp, *Lincoln*, 15–17; E. Foner, *Fiery Trial*, 4, 17–18; Wieck, *Lincoln's Quest*, 9; Clay, "Petitions for the Abolition of Slavery . . . February 7, 1839," in Mallory, ed., *Life and Speeches*, 2:355–75; Sinha, *Slave's Cause*, 87–91.
3. E. Foner, *Fiery Trial*, 6, 8; Hagedorn, *Beyond the River*; Yannessa, *Coffin*.
4. Lincoln to A. G. Hodges, April 4, 1864, *Collected Works*, 7:281.
5. Moore, *Missouri Controversy*; American Convention, *Minutes of the Proceedings*, 42–43 (quotation); Forbes, *Missouri Compromise*, 2–3, 33–120.
6. J. M. Peck to H. Warren, March 27, 1823, Governors's Message, November 16, 1824, in Alvord, ed., *Coles*, 334–36 (1st quotation), 355–56 (2nd quotation); Dillon, *Abolitionists*, 23–24; Vaux to Coles, May 27, 1823, in Washburne, *Coles*, 152–53 (2nd quotation).
7. Burlingame, *Lincoln*, 1:123 (1st quotation); Berwanger, *Frontier against Slavery*, 26–27 (2nd quotation), 32; *Liberator*, April 3, 1840 (3rd quotation).
8. E. Foner, *Fiery Trial*, 14; Lincoln to A. G. Hodges, April 4, 1864, *Collected Works*, 7:281; Gienapp, *Lincoln*, 3–23, 37; Burlingame, *Lincoln*, 1:71–72, 81–83, 87–91, 103–23, 143–47, 161–66.
9. Wiltse, *New Nation*, 1–123; Remini, *Jackson*, 100–142.
10. Freehling, *Road to Disunion*, 1:560–61; Howe, *Political Culture of the American Whigs*, 13, 17–18, 150–58; Walters, *American Reformers*, 21–29.
11. Mintz, *Moralists and Modernizers*; Dillon, *Lundy*, 42 (quotation); Staudenraus, *African Colonization Movement*; Burin, *Slavery and the Peculiar Solution*; E. Foner, *Fiery Trial*, 14, 18–19; Burlingame, *Inner World*, 30.
12. Peter Bestes et al. to Sir, April 20, 1773, in Nash, *Race and Revolution*, 173–74 (quotation); Horton and Horton, *In Hope of Liberty*, 178, 181–88, 191, 208–9.
13. Newman, *Transformation of American Abolitionism*, 96–104; Stewart, *Holy Warriors*, 37–47.
14. Mayer, *All on Fire*, 3–151; Stewart, *Garrison*, 1–98; Thomas, *Liberator*, 3–154.

15. "Declaration of Sentiments of the American Anti-Slavery Society," *Liberator*, December 14, 1833 (quotation); Wyatt-Brown, "Abolitionists' Postal Campaign of 1835," 227–38.

16. Filler, *Crusade against Slavery*, 66–67; Burlingame, *Lincoln*, 1:122–25; E. Foner, *Fiery Trial*, 14–19, 22–24, 35–36; Volpe, *Forlorn Hope of Freedom*, 4–5; Gienapp, *Lincoln*, 4, 41; William H. Herndon to Truman H. Bartlett, July 8, 1887, in Hertz, ed., *Hidden Lincoln*, 188.

17. Sewell, *Ballots for Freedom*, 63–64; Howe, *Political Culture of the American Whigs*, 17–18; Price, "Ohio Anti-Slavery Convention of 1836," 182; Ohio Anti-Slavery Society, *Report of the Second Anniversary*, 9; Cooper, *South and the Politics of Slavery*, 53–54; Huggins, *Mangum*, 59–106; Remini, *Clay*, 507–11.

18. Burlingame, *Lincoln*, 1:108, 110, 154–55; E. Foner, *Fiery Trial*, 31.

19. "Protest in Illinois Legislature on Slavery," March 3, 1837, *Collected Works*, 1:74–75 (quotations); Burlingame, *Lincoln*, 1:122–25; E. Foner, *Fiery Trial*, 24–26; Gienapp, *Lincoln*, 8–9; Sinha, "Allies for Emancipation?," in Foner, ed., *Our Lincoln*, 170.

20. E. Foner, *Fiery Trial*, 23; Dillon, *Lovejoy*, 1–14, 68–70 (quotation), 129–42; Bowen, "Anti-Slavery Convention," 329–56.

21. "Address before the Young Men's Lyceum of Springfield, Illinois, January 27, 1838," *Collected Works*, 1:109–13 (1st and 2nd quotations); Wieck, *Lincoln's Quest*, 32 (3rd quotation).

22. Burlingame, *Lincoln*, 1:42–44, 56; John Hanks interview [1865–66], in Wilson and Davis, eds., *Herndon's Informants*, 457 (quotation); Campanella, *Lincoln in New Orleans*; E. Foner, *Fiery Trial*, 8–12.

23. Burlingame, *Lincoln*, 1:146; Harrold, *Border War*, 77–79; Huston, "Experiential Basis," 609–40.

2. Different Paths

1. Stewart, "Peaceful Hopes and Violent Experiences," 293–309; Harrold, *Rise of Aggressive Abolitionism*, 7–8.

2. Stewart, "Peaceful Hopes and Violent Experiences," 304–9; Stewart, *Holy Warriors*, 103, 113–14, 121–22, 132, 152, 155, 161, 169.

3. Friedman, *Gregarious Saints*, 68–95; McKivigan, *War against Proslavery Religion*, 75–84.

4. Harrold, *Abolitionists and the South*, 7, 72–77, 127–30, 140–44; Wiecek, *Sources of Antislavery Constitutionalism*, 202–27; Blue, *Chase*, 61–64.

5. Lincoln to Durley, October 3, 1845, *Collected Works*, 1:347–48.

6. Willard, "Personal Reminiscences of Life in Illinois," 86 (quotation); Hart, "Underground Railroad"; Burlingame, *Lincoln*, 1:250–52, 380–81; Weik, *Real Lincoln*, 196–98; Blue, *Chase*, 31–40.

7. E. Foner, *Fiery Trial*, 50.

8. Lincoln to Durley, October 3, 1845, *Collected Works*, 1:347–48 (quotations); Bemis, *Adams*, 355–56; Adams to Lundy, May 12, 20, 1836, Adams Papers.

9. Schroeder, *Mr. Polk's War*, 29–32; Burlingame, *Lincoln*, 1:250; Oates, *Lincoln*, 61.

10. Gienapp, *Lincoln*, 34–35; Remini, *Clay*, 692–93 (quotation).

11. Burlingame, *Lincoln*, 1:259–61 (quotation); E. Foner, *Fiery Trial*, 51.

12. Stewart, *Holy Warriors*, 113–14; Smith to *Albany Patriot*, May 8, 1847, in William and Smith, *Address of the Macedon Convention*, 14 (1st quotation); Harrold, *Bailey*, 77; Giddings, *Speeches in Congress*, 191, 193 (2nd and 3rd quotations).

13. Burlingame, *Lincoln*, 1:265 (1st quotation); "Speech in the United States House of Representatives: The War with Mexico," January 13, 1848, "Speech at Wilmington, Delaware," June 10, 1848, Lincoln to Linder, March 22, 1848, "Speech in U.S. House of Representatives on the Presidential Question," July 27, 1848, *Collected Works*, 1:432 (2nd quotation), 476 (3rd quotation), 458 (4th quotation), 476, 515 (5th quotation).

14. Burlingame, *Lincoln*, 1:284–87; Burlingame, *Inner World*, 28–29; E. Foner, *Fiery Trial*, 51–52; C.B.A. to *Tribune*, September 20, 1849, in *New-York Daily Tribune*, September 22, 1849 (1st quotation); Julian, *Giddings*, 261 (2nd and 3rd quotations).

15. Burlingame, *Lincoln*, 1:284; Harrold, *Subversives*, 108–11.

16. Harrold, *Subversives*, 116–45. There is no mention of the *Pearl* in Lincoln's *Collected Works*, 1:462–69.

17. Burlingame, *Lincoln*, 1:287; *Journal of the House of Representatives*, 30th Cong., 2nd Sess. (December 21, 1848), 132–33; *Congressional Globe*, 30th Cong., 2nd Sess. (January 10, 1849), app. 214; Julian, *Giddings*, 261.

18. "Remarks and Resolution Introduced into the United States House of Representative concerning Abolition of Slavery in the District of Columbia," January 10, 1849, *Collected Works*, 2:20–22 (1st and 2nd quotations), 22n4 (3rd quotation); *Liberator*, July 13, 1860 (4th and 5th quotations).

19. Holt, *Rise and Fall*, 215; Burlingame, *Lincoln*, 1:273–74; E. Foner, *Fiery Trial*, 52; Sewell, *Ballots for Freedom*, 139–69.

20. Sewell, *Ballots for Freedom*, 150, 162–64, 170–81; Potter, *Impending Crisis*, 70–72, 77, 81.

21. Burlingame, *Lincoln*, 1:277–81.

22. "Speech in U.S. House of Representatives on the Presidential Question," July 27, 1848, "Speech at Worcester, Massachusetts," September 12, 1848, "Speech at Lacon, Illinois," November 1, 1848, *Illinois State Register*, October 27, 1848, *Collected Works*, 1:505, 2:1–4 (1st quotation), 2:11–14 (2nd quotation).

23. Wyatt-Brown, *Tappan*, 280–81 (1st quotation); Whittier to Tappan, July 14, 1849, in S. Pickard, *Life and Letters of Whittier*, 1:337; Garrison to Samuel May Jr., December 2, 1848, in Merrill and Ruchames, eds., *Letters of Garrison*, 3:604 (2nd–5th quotations); *North Star*, May 25, 1848 (6th–9th quotations).

24. *Collected Works*, 2:31–63, 71–79; Burlingame, *Lincoln*, 1:294–308.

3. Limited Convergence

1. *Congressional Globe*, 31st Cong., 1st Sess. (January 29, 1850), 244–47; Hamilton, *Prologue to Conflict*, 133–65.

2. Potter, *Impending Crisis*, 90–120, 132; Blue, *Free Soilers*, 181.

3. "Eulogy Pronounced by Hon. A. Lincoln, on the Life and Services of the Late President of the United States," July 25 1850, *Collected Works*, 2:83–89 (quotation); Gienapp, *Lincoln*, 40–45.

4. For a discussion of the cases Lincoln avoided, see Weik, *Real Lincoln*, 198 (1st quotation). See also Lincoln to Salmon P. Chase, June 20, 1859, Lincoln to Alonzo J. Glover, January 15, 1860, *Collected Works*, 3:386, 514. For a look at the charges Lincoln made against Pierce, see "Speech to the Springfield Scott Club," August 14, 26, 1852, *Collected Works*, 2:156–57. For a glance at the criticisms Lincoln made, see R. Browne, *Lincoln and the Men of His Time*, 1:517 (2nd quotation); F. Browne, *Everyday Life of Lincoln*, 248–49 (3rd quotation); Lincoln to Speed, August 24, 1855, in Gienapp, ed., *This Fiery Trial*, 35 (4th quotation).

5. "Whig Party Platform of 1852," June 17, 1852 (http://www.presidency.ucsb.edu/ws/?pid=25856), and "1852 Democratic Party Platform," June 1, 1852 (http://www.presidency.ucsb.edu/ws/?pid=29575), in Woolley and Peters, *American Presidency Project*; Mayfield, *Rehearsal for Republicanism*, 175–76; Harrold, *Border War*, 147–49.

6. Harrold, *Border War*, 155–56; "Eulogy on Henry Clay," July 6, 1852, *Collected Works*, 2:123, 127–30.

7. "Eulogy on Henry Clay," July 6, 1852, *Collected Works*, 2:130–32.

8. E. Foner, *Fiery Trial*, 123–29; Garrison et al. to Louis Kossuth, [February 1852], in Merrill and Ruchames, eds., *Letters of Garrison*, 4:169 (1st–4th quotations); "The Colonizationist Revival: An Address Delivered in Boston, Massachusetts, on 31 May 1849," in Blassingame et al., eds., *Douglass Papers*, series 1, 2:206 (5th–7th quotations).

9. Birney to Douglass, n.d., *Frederick Douglass' Paper*, April 8, 1852; Delany, "The Condition, Elevation, Emigration, and Destiny of the Colored People of the United States, Politically Considered," in Moses, ed., *Classical Black Nationalism*, 112 (quotation); *National Era*, January 21, 1858, April 1, 1858, May 31, 1858, June 10, 1858, February 24, 1859.

10. Mayer, *All on Fire*, 438–40; "Slavery, Freedom, and the Kansas-Nebraska Act: An Address Delivered in Chicago, Illinois, on 30 October 1854," *Douglass Papers*, series 1, 2:538–59 (1st and 2nd quotations); Smith to Douglass, August 28, 1854, in Smith, *Speeches of Smith*, 401 (3rd quotation); Wyatt-Brown, *Tappan*, 332 (4th quotation); McDaniel, *Problem of Democracy*, 210. Blassingame et al., eds., *Douglass Papers*, series 1, vol. 2 contains no mention of Lincoln.

11. R. Johnson, *Liberty Party*, 98, 148, 187–88, 200; American and Foreign Anti-Slavery Society, *[Eighth] Annual Report*, 3; Niven et al., eds., *Chase Papers*, 1:296–97, 318–21, 335–36, 352–53, 390–91, 394–95, 2:6–7, 8–10; *Congressional Globe*, 33rd Cong., 1st Sess. (January 30, 1854), 281–82 (quotations).

12. Gienapp, *Lincoln*, 50–52; R. Johnson, *Liberty Party*, 333, 339, 358; Codding, "Biographical Sketch," 169–96; Volpe, *Forlorn Hope of Freedom*, 14, 69, 114; Magdol, *Lovejoy*, 12–13; "Speech at Peoria, Illinois, October 16, 1854," *Collected Works*, 2:275, 278.

13. Burlingame, *Lincoln*, 1:364, 370 (1st and 2nd quotations); Gienapp, *Origins of the Republican Party*, 123–24 (3rd quotation and my emphasis); E. Foner, *Fiery Trial*, 73–75. The first and second quotations are from an anonymous editorial published in the *Illinois Daily Journal*, March 24, 1854, that Burlingame attributes to Lincoln.

14. "Speech at Winchester, Illinois," August 26, 1854, "Speech at Bloomington, Illinois," September 12, 1854, *Collected Works*, 2:226–27 (quotation), 230–33.

15. "Speech at Springfield," October 4, 1854, "Speech at Peoria," October 16, 1854, *Collected Works*, 2:240–83 (quotations); Burlingame, *Lincoln*, 1:376–89; E. Foner, *Fiery Trial*, 69.

16. Burlingame, *Lincoln*, 1:375–76.

17. Codding to Lincoln, November 13, 1854, Lincoln Papers; Lincoln to Codding, November 27, 1854, *Collected Works*, 2:288 (quotations).

18. *Free West*, November 30, 1854, December 14, 1854; Elihu B. Washburne to Lincoln, December 19, 20, 1854, Jesse O. Norton to Lincoln, December 12, 20, 1854, Lincoln Papers; Blanchard, *Discovery and Conquests*, 670–71; "Drafts of Resolutions Recommending Amendment of the Kansas-Nebraska Act," [January 4, 1855?], *Collected Works*, 2:300–301 (quotations); Burlingame, *Lincoln*, 1:396; Gienapp, *Lincoln*, 53–54.

19. Harrold, *Border War*, 162–69; Perry, *Radical Abolitionism*, 240–41; Friedman, *Gregarious Saints*, 206.

20. Lincoln to George Robertson, August 15, 1855, Lincoln to Speed, August 14, 1855, *Collected Works*, 2:318 (1st, 2nd, 5th, and 6th quotations), 320–23 (3rd and 4th quotations); Parker to William H. Seward, May 19, 1854, in Weiss, *Parker*, 2:206.

21. Lincoln to Lovejoy, August 11, 1855, *Collected Works*, 2:316–17; Burlingame, *Lincoln*, 1:408–9, 411–12; Gienapp, *Origins of the Republican Party*, 286–89.

22. Gienapp, *Origins of the Republican Party*, 289; Whitney, *Lincoln the Citizen*, 259–61.

23. Burlingame, *Lincoln*, 1:418–19; "Speech at Springfield," June 10, 1856, *Collected Works*, 2:344–45 (quotations).

24. Dean Grodzins, "Why Theodore Parker Backed John Brown: The Political and Social Roots of Support for Abolitionist Violence," in Russo and Finkelman, eds., *Terrible Swift Sword*, 3–22; Dean Grodzins, "Theodore Parker vs. John S. Rock on the Anglo-Saxon and the African," in Lowance, ed., *House Divided*, 299–310; Herndon to Jesse W. Weik, October 28, 1885, in Hertz, ed., *Hidden Lincoln*, 96; Herndon and Weik, *Herndon's Lincoln*, 2:362–63; Donald, *Lincoln's Herndon*, 74; E. Foner, *Fiery Trial*, 87–88; Donald, *Lincoln's Herndon*, 75.

25. Herndon and Weik, *Herndon's Lincoln*, 2:363; Herndon to Weik, October 28, 1885, in Hertz, ed., *Hidden Lincoln*, 96; Newton, *Lincoln and Herndon*, 72–74, 76–78; Herndon to Parker, February 13, 1855, November 23, 1858, in Newton, *Lincoln and Herndon*, 76 (1st and 2nd quotations), 241 (3rd quotation); Wieck, *Lincoln's Quest*, 24–25.

4. Lincoln Keeps His Distance

1. Wieck, *Lincoln's Quest*, 14; Guelzo, *Lincoln*, 206–7.

2. Trefousse, *Radial Republicans*, 8, 16; Seward to Samuel Joseph May, November 9, 1855, Seward Papers; Trefousse, *Radical Republicans*, 12–13; Chase to Gerrit Smith, February 15, 1856, Chase Papers; Giddings to Thomas Wentworth Higginson, January 7, 1857, *Liberator*, January 23, 1857; Sumner to Smith, March 18, 1856, in Pierce, *Sumner*, 3:433; Wilson to Higginson, January 10, 1857, *Liberator*, January 23, 1857; Theodore Parker to Horace Mann, June 27, 1856, in Weiss, *Parker*, 2:297–98.

3. "Republican Party Platform of 1856," June 18, 1856 (http://www.presidency.ucsb.edu/ws/?pid=29619), in Woolley and Peters, *American Presidency Project*; P. Foner, ed., *Life and Writings of Douglass*, 2:392.

4. *Daily Illinois State Register*, June 12, 1856, "Speech at Kalamazoo," August 27, 1856, "Speech at Petersburg," August 30, 1856, *Collected Works*, 2:344 (1st quotation), 356 (3rd and fourth quotations), 365 (2nd quotation).

5. Lincoln to David Davis, July 7, 1856, *Collected Works, First Supplement*, 27; Magdol, *Lovejoy*, 158.

6. Burlingame, *Lincoln*, 1:421, 430–31; "Speech at Galena," July 23, 1856, "Speech at Kalamazoo, Michigan," August 27, 1856, "Speech at Vandalia," September 23, 1856, *Collected Works*, 2:354, 361 (2nd and 3rd quotations), 377–79 (1st quotation).

7. "Speech at Bloomington," May 29, 1856, "Speech at Kalamazoo," August 27, 1856, "Speech at Belleville," October 18, 1856, *Collected Works*, 2:341 (1st quotation), 361 (2nd quotation), 379–80 (3rd quotation).

8. Gienapp, *Origins of the Republican Party*, 413–15; Dublin, ed., *United States Congressional Elections*, 176–78.

9. Burlingame, *Lincoln*, 1:433–34; Gienapp, *Origins of the Republican Party*, illustration no. 16 (between 414 and 415); Gienapp, *Lincoln*, 57; "Notes for Speech at Chicago, Illinois," February 28, 1857, *Collected Works*, 2:391 (quotation); Parker to Herndon, November 17, 1856, in Newton, *Lincoln and Herndon*, 100–101; Harrold, *Border War*, 166, 190–91; Scott, *Secret Six*, 200–201, 228.

10. "Speech at Kalamazoo," August 27, 1856, "Speech at Vandalia," September 23, 1856, "First Debate with Stephen A. Douglas, at Ottawa, Illinois," August 21, 1858, *Collected Works*, 2:362–63, 378 (1st quotation), 3:29 (4th quotation); "Speech at a Republican Banquet," December 10, 1856, in Gienapp, ed., *This Fiery Trial*, 38–39 (2nd and 3rd quotations).

11. "Speech at a Republican Banquet," December 10, 1856, in Gienapp, ed., *This Fiery Trial*, 38–39 (1st–3rd quotations); "Fragment on Stephen A. Douglas," [December 1856?], *Collected Works*, 2:383 (4th quotation); Burlingame, *Inner World*, 27.

12. Fehrenbacher, *Dred Scott Case*, 347 (quotation); Harrold, *Bailey*, 197–98; Harlow, *Smith*, 369; Quarles, *Black Abolitionists*, 231–32.

13. "Speech at Springfield," June 26, 1857, *Collected Works*, 2:403–10; Sinha, "Allies for Emancipation?," in Foner, ed., *Our Lincoln*, 173.

14. "Speech at Springfield," June 26, 1857, *Collected Works*, 2:409; Sinha, *Slave's Cause*, 574–80.

15. Newton, *Lincoln and Herndon*, 98–99, 124; Burlingame, *Lincoln*, 1:367; Commager, *Parker*, 250.

16. Commager, *Parker*, 250, 261; Parker, *Present Aspect of Slavery*, 41–42, 44; *Liberator*, February 19, 1858; Parker to Eli Thayer, February 26, 1858, Thayer Papers; Parker to Mann, June 27, 1856, in Weiss, *Parker*, 2:188 (quotation). Examples of Parker's correspondence with Republicans include Parker to Sumner, January 14, 1856, Parker to Seward, May 19, 1854, Parker to Banks, October 23, 1855, Parker to Chase, March 16, 1854, Parker to Hale, February 23, 1856, in Weiss, *Parker*, 2:157–60, 206–7, 223–26.

17. Herndon to Parker, June 17, July 4, 29, 1857, in Newton, *Lincoln and Herndon*, 117–23 (quotation); Herndon to Parker, June 29, 1857, in Wieck, *Lincoln's Quest*, 68.

18. Herndon to Parker, October 30, 1855, Herndon to Parker, July 4, 29, 1857, in Newton, *Lincoln and Herndon*, 82–83 (quotation), 122–23; Gienapp, *Lincoln*, 58.

19. Burlingame, *Lincoln*, 1:445–52; Gienapp, *Lincoln*, 59–60; Herndon to Parker, December 26, 1857, in Newton, *Lincoln and Herndon*, 136 (quotation).

20. Lincoln to Trumbull, December 28, 1857, Lincoln to Elihu B. Washburne, April 26, 1858, May 10, 15, 27, 1858, Lincoln to Jediah F. Alexander, May 15, 1858, *Collected Works*, 2:430, 443–47, 455; Herndon to Jesse W. Weik, December 23, 1885, in Hertz, ed., *Hidden Lincoln*, 114 (quotation); Burlingame, *Lincoln*, 1:447–53; Wieck, *Lincoln's Quest*, 63–65; Commager, *Parker*, 266; Herndon to Parker, May 29, 1858, in Newton, *Lincoln and Herndon*, 162; Herndon to Weik, April 14, 1885, December 23, 1885, in Hertz, ed., *Hidden Lincoln*, 94, 113–15.

21. Newton, *Lincoln and Herndon*, 124–25, 158–59.

22. Gienapp, *Lincoln*, 59–60; Burlingame, *Lincoln*, 1:457–61; Egerton, *Year of Meteors*, 44–47; "'A House Divided' Speech to the Republican State Convention, June 16, 1858," in Gienapp, ed., *This Fiery Trial*, 43–44 (quotation).

23. Glickstein, "Chattelization of Northern Whites," 48 (1st and 2nd quotations); Nevins, *Ordeal of the Union*, 2:78 (3rd quotation); "Slavery, Freedom, and the Kansas-Nebraska Act: An Address Delivered in Chicago, Illinois, on 30 October 1854," in Blassingame et al., eds., *Douglass Papers*, series 1, 2:544 (4th quotation); Parker, *Sermon of the Dangers*, 31 (5th and 6th quotations).

24. *Liberator*, October 15, 1858; Burlingame, *Lincoln*, 1:468, 521; "Speech of Senator Douglas," July 9, 1858, in Copeland, ed., *Antebellum Era*, 393 (1st quotation); Johannsen, ed., *Lincoln-Douglas Debates*, 42 (2nd and 3rd quotations); Newton, *Lincoln and Herndon*, 188–89 (4th quotation); *Daily Illinois State Register*, October 8, 1858, in Sparks, ed., *Collections*, 3:526 (5th quotation).

25. "Speech at Chicago," July 10, 1858, "First Debate with Douglas," August 21, 1858, *Collected Works*, 2:492 (1st quotation), 3:29 (5th quotation); "Sixth Debate, at Quincy, October 13, 1858," "Seventh Debate, at Alton, October 15, 1858," "Last Debate of the Campaign, October 30, 1858," in Gienapp, ed., *This Fiery Trial*, 55–56, 58–60 (6th quotation), 60–61 (2nd–4th quotations), 67–68; Kaplan, *Lincoln and the Abolitionists*, 215–17.

26. "Seventh Debate, at Alton, October 15, 1858," in Gienapp, ed., *This Fiery Trial*, 60–63 (1st quotation); "Sixth Joint Debate, October 13, 1858 at Quincy, Illinois," *Collected Works*, 3:249–50 (2nd quotation).

27. Wieck, *Lincoln's Quest*, 43–44, 68; Parker to Herndon, July 1, 1858, Parker to Herndon, August 28, 1858, in Newton, *Lincoln and Herndon*, 177 (1st quotation), 197, 201 (2nd quotation), 202; "Freedom in the West Indies: An Address Delivered in Poughkeepsie, New York, on 2 August 1858," in Blassingame et al., eds., *Douglass Papers*, series 1, 3:233–37 (3rd

and 4th quotations); Sinha, "Allies for Emancipation?," in Foner, ed., *Our Lincoln*, 171.

28. Wright to Friends, July 18, 1858, *Liberator*, July 30, 1858 (1st and 2nd quotations); *Free South*, qtd. in *Liberator*, October 15, 1858, November 5, 1858; Stevens, *Reporter's Lincoln*, 86 (3rd quotation); "Speech of H. Ford Douglass [*sic*]," *Liberator*, July 13, 1860 (4th quotation). See also Norman, "Other Lincoln-Douglas Debate," 1–21.

29. "Mr. Douglas' Speech," in "First Debate with Douglas," August 21, 1858, *Collected Works*, 3:3–5; Parker to Herndon, September 9, 1858, Herndon to Parker, September 11, 1858, in Newton, *Lincoln and Herndon*, 206–7 (1st–3rd quotations), 209 (4th quotation); Commager, *Parker*, 272–309.

30. *Anti-Slavery Bugle*, September 4, 1858.

5. National Impact

1. Burlingame, *Lincoln*, 1:551–56, 559.

2. "Speech at Chicago, Illinois," March 1, 1859, Lincoln to Mark W. Delahay, May 14, 1859, Lincoln to Nathan Sargent, June 23, 1859, "Speech at Dayton, Ohio," September 17, 1859; "Speech at Cincinnati, Ohio," September 17, 1859, *Collected Works*, 3:369–70 (2nd quotation), 379 (1st quotation), 387–88, 436–52 (3rd quotation); E. Foner, *Fiery Trial*, 112–17.

3. Lincoln to Elihu B. Washburne, January 29, 1859, Lincoln to Chase, June 9, 1859, "Fragments: Notes for Speeches," [September 1859?], "Speech at Columbus, Ohio," September 16, 1859, *Collected Works*, 3:351 (1st quotation), 384, 399 (2nd quotation), 401–2.

4. Harrold, *Rise of Aggressive Abolitionism*, 141–42; Harrold, *Border War*, 138–58, 164–73; Harrold, *Abolitionists and the South*, 53.

5. [Smith], "A Letter to the American Slaves from Those Who Have Fled from American Slavery," *North Star*, September 15, 1850 (1st quotation); *Liberator*, February 13, 1857 (2nd quotation); "Disunion Convention," October 28, 1857, *Liberator*, November 6, 1857 (3rd quotation).

6. Harrold, *Rise of Aggressive Abolitionism*, 143; Gates, ed., *Douglass Autobiographies*, 717–19 (1st and 2nd quotations); Scott, *Secret Six*, 199–269; Smith, circular letter, *National Era*, September 15, 1859 (3rd and 4th quotations).

7. Oates, *To Purge This Land*, 290–306; Reynolds, *Brown*, 288–333.

8. *Liberator*, October 28, 1859 (1st–5th quotations); "Speech of Wm. Lloyd Garrison, at the Meeting in Tremont Temple, Dec. 2d, relating to the Execution of John Brown," *Liberator*, December 16, 1859 (6th quotation).

9. "The Puritan Principle and John Brown," in Phillips, *Speeches, Lectures, and Letters*, 2nd series, 308 (1st and 2nd quotations); Douglass to *Democrat and American* (Rochester, N.Y.), October 31, 1859, in P. Foner, ed., *Life and Writings of Douglass*, 2:460–63 (3rd quotation); *Douglass*

Monthly 2 (November 1859), in P. Foner, ed., *Douglass*, 374–75 (4th–6th quotations); Child to Mary Stearns, November 3 1859, Stutler Collection; Parker to Francis Jackson, November 24, 1859, in Commager, ed., *Parker*, 267 (7th and 8th quotations).

10. Burlingame, *Lincoln*, 1:574; "Speech at Elwood, Kansas," December 1 (November 30?), 1859, "Speech at Leavenworth, Kansas," December 3, 1859, *Collected Works*, 3:495–96 (1st–4th quotations), 502 (5th quotation). See also Reynolds, *Brown*, 357, 427–30; Burlingame, *Lincoln*, 1:575–76; Chase to H. H. Barrett, October 29, 1859, in Niven et al., eds., *Chase Papers*, 3:22–23.

11. "On the Invasion of States," U.S. Senate, January 23, 1860, in Flint, *Life of Douglas*, app. 160 (1st quotation); Reynolds, *Brown*, 425–26; *New York Herald*, May 22, 1860 (2nd quotation), *St. Louis Democrat*, November 8, 1860, qtd. in *New-York Daily Tribune*, November 12, 1860 (3rd quotation).

12. "Speech at the Cooper Union," February 27, 1860, in Gienapp, ed., *This Fiery Trial*, 72–80. See also "Second Speech at Leavenworth, Kansas," December 5, 1859, "Speech at Dover, New Hampshire," March 2, 1860, *Collected Works*, 3:503, 553.

13. Garrison to J. Miller McKim, October 14, 1856, Garrison to Parker Pillsbury, June 3, 1859, Garrison to Abigail Kelley Foster, September 8, 1859, in Merrill and Ruchames, eds., *Letters of Garrison*, 4:410, 627–29, 649–53; Stewart, *Holy Warriors*, 173–74; John G. Whittier to Sumner, November 15, 1853, in J. Pickard, ed., *Letters of Whittier*, 2:238–39; Massachusetts Anti-Slavery Society, *Twenty-First Annual Report*, 86–87, 96–98; Parker to Chase, March 16, 1854, in Weiss, *Parker*, 2:226; Abbott, *Cobbler in Congress*, 75; Smith to Chase, April 20, 1856, Chase Papers; Henry C. Wright to Giddings, February 2, 1857, Giddings Papers.

14. *Liberator*, September 16, 1859 (quotation); Lydia Maria Child to Whittier, n.d., in Baer, *Heart Is Like Heaven*, 260; "Speech at Hartford, Connecticut," March 5, 1860, *Collected Works*, 4:5–6.

15. Burlingame, *Lincoln*, 1:601–11, 619–28; Gienapp, *Lincoln*, 69–70.

16. Burlingame, *Lincoln*, 1:612–13; Stewart, *Giddings*, 271–72.

17. Lincoln to Clay, May 26, July 20, August 10, 1860, *Collected Works*, 4:53–54, 85, 92.

18. May 21, 1862, entry, in Scarborough, ed., *Diary of Edmund Ruffin*, 1:421 (1st quotation); *Charleston (S.C.) Mercury*, October 15, 1860 (2nd–4th quotations); Burlingame, *Lincoln*, 1:630 (5th quotation); *Daily Illinois State Register*, August 24, 1860 (6th and 7th quotations).

19. "Speech of Wendell Phillips . . . May 30th, 1860," *Liberator*, June 8, 1860 (1st quotation); "Abraham Lincoln, the Slave-Hound of Illinois," *Liberator*, June 22, 1860 (2nd quotation); Garrison to Johnson, August

9, 1860, in Merrill and Ruchames, eds., *Letters of Garrison*, 4:687 (3rd and 4th quotation); Mayer, *All on Fire*, 507–9; *National Anti-Slavery Standard*, June 2, 1860.

20. "Political Anti-Slavery Convention," *Liberator*, June 15, 1860 (1st quotation); "'Independence Day' Anti-Slavery Celebration at Framingham," *Liberator*, July 20, 1860 (2nd quotation); *National Anti-Slavery Standard*, October 13, 1860 (3rd quotation). See also Stewart, *Phillips*, 210; Robertson, *Pillsbury*, 120–22; Sinha, "Allies for Emancipation?," in Foner, ed., *Our Lincoln*, 175–76.

21. *Principia*, June 2, 1860 (1st and 2nd quotations); J. B. Edwards to Smith, June 13, July 11, 1860, qtd. in Harlow, *Smith*, 428 (3rd quotation); *Liberator*, September 7, 1860 (4th quotation).

22. *Douglass Monthly* 3 (June 1860), 276 (1st quotation); "Slavery and the Irrepressible Conflict: An Address Delivered at Geneva, New York, on 1 August 1860," in Blassingame et al., eds., *Douglass Papers*, series 1, 3:381–82 (2nd–4th quotations); *Douglass Monthly* 3 (August 1860), 306 (5th quotation); Smith to Giddings, June 2, 1860, Giddings Papers (6th quotation). See also J. McPherson, *Struggle for Equality*, 18–19.

23. "Speech of H. Ford Douglass [*sic*]," *Liberator*, July 13, 1860 (1st–4th quotation); "Proceedings of the Eighteenth Anniversary of the Western Anti-Slavery Society: Sunday Morning Session. Speech of H. Ford Douglass [*sic*]," *Anti-Slavery Bugle*, October 6, 1860 (5th–7th quotations). See also Burlingame, *Lincoln*, 1:634, 637; Kaplan, *Lincoln and the Abolitionists*, 246–47.

24. *Liberator*, September 28, 1860 (1st and 2nd quotations); Johnson to J. Miller McKim, October 11, 1860, May Antislavery Collection (3rd quotation).

25. J. McPherson, *Struggle for Equality*, 14; d'Entremont, *Southern Emancipator*, 149 (quotations); Johnson, "American Missionary Association," 218–19; Harrold, *Border War*, 191–93; *Liberator*, June 15, 1860; Logan, "Bailey."

26. Burlingame, *Lincoln*, 1:638; Goodheart, *Abolitionist*, 136–37, 151; Whittier to Chase, October 30, 1860, in J. Pickard, ed., *Letters of Whittier*, 2:474 (quotation).

27. Whittier to Chase, November 9, 1860, Chase Papers (1st quotation); *Douglass Monthly* 3 (December 1860), 370–71 (2nd and 3rd quotations); Wright, *Eye Opener*, 52–54 (4th–6th quotations); *National Anti-Slavery Standard*, November 17, 1860 (7th–10th quotations).

28. Phillips, *Speeches, Lectures, and Letters*, 2nd series, 294–318.

29. Burlingame, *Lincoln*, 1:575 (quotation), 638; Sewell, *Ballots for Freedom*, 346–55; Trefousse, *Radical Republicans*, 130; Reynolds, *Brown*, 424–26; Mayer, *All on Fire*, 505.

6. Contentious Relationship

1. *Collected Works*, 4:91, 142–44, 162, 182, 193–97; *Illinois Daily State Journal*, December 18, 1860; Herndon to Samuel Sewall, February 1, 1861, Garrison Papers (1st quotation); *Liberator*, February 15, 1861 (2nd quotation).

2. Lincoln to Lyman Trumbull, November 20, 1860, Lincoln to Raymond, December 18, 1860, Lincoln to Stephens, December 22, 1860, Lincoln to Seward, February 1, 1861, *Collected Works*, 4:141–42 (1st quotation), 156 (2nd quotation), 160 (3rd quotation), 183 (4th quotation).

3. Smith to Chase, December 18, 1860, Smith Papers (1st and 2nd quotations); Phillips, *Speeches, Lectures, and Letters*, 362 (3rd–5th quotations).

4. "First Inaugural Address—First Edition and Revisions," *Collected Works*, 4:250–61 (1st–5th quotations); *National Anti-Slavery Standard*, March 9, 1861 (6th quotation); Child to John G. Whittier, January 21, 1862, in Holland and Meltzer, eds., *Collected Correspondence of Child* (7th quotation); *Douglass Monthly* 3 (April 1861), 475 (8th–10th quotations).

5. *Liberator*, March 8, 1861.

6. Gienapp, *Lincoln*, 82–87.

7. "Proclamation Calling Militia and Convening Congress," April 15, 1861, *Collected Works*, 4:332 (quotation); J. McPherson, *Struggle for Equality*, 58; "Message to Congress in Special Session," July 4, 1861, *Collected Works*, 4:439.

8. J. McPherson, *Struggle for Equality*, 52–54; Garrison to Johnson, April 19, 1861, in Merrill and Ruchames, eds., *Letters of Garrison*, 5:16–17 (quotation).

9. "Under the Flag: A Discourse Delivered in the Music Hall, Boston, April 21, 1861," in Phillips, *Speeches, Lectures, and Letters*, 397, 400, 402, 408, 411–12 (1st–7th quotations); *Liberator*, July 12, 1861 (8th quotation). See also Sinha, "Allies for Emancipation?," in Foner, ed., *Our Lincoln*, 179.

10. *Principia*, May 4, 1861 (1st and 2nd quotations), December 21, 1861 (3rd quotation); J. McPherson, *Struggle for Equality*, 61–63, 81–83; "Under the Flag," in Phillips, *Speeches, Lectures, and Letters*, 409–13; Smith, *Smith to Lovejoy*; Garrison, ed., *Abolition of Slavery*. See also Sinha, "Allies for Emancipation?," in Foner, ed., *Our Lincoln*, 179; Kaplan, *Lincoln and the Abolitionists*, 299.

11. J. McPherson, *Struggle for Equality*, 56; Bassett to Smith, May 9, 1861, Smith Papers (1st quotation); "Fourth of July Celebration at Framingham," *Liberator*, July 12, 1861; *Douglass Monthly* 4 (August 1861), in P. Foner, ed., *Douglass*, 464–65 (2nd quotation); Child to Henrietta Sargent, July 26, 1861, in Child, *Letters of Child*, 153–54 (3rd quotation); *National Anti-Slavery Standard*, August 24, 1861 (4th and 5th quotations).

12. J. McPherson, *Struggle for Equality*, 70–72.
13. Smith to Lincoln, August 31, 1861, *Liberator*, September 13, 1861 (1st quotation); Conway to Charles Sumner, September 17, 1861, Sumner Papers (2nd quotation); Burlingame, *Lincoln*, 2:202–5, 210–11.
14. *Liberator*, September 20, 1861 (1st and 2nd quotations); Garrison to Johnson, October 7, 1861, in Merrill and Ruchames, eds., *Letters of Garrison*, 5:37 (3rd quotation); Conway to Sumner, September 17, 1861, Sumner Papers (4th quotation); *Douglass Monthly* 4 (October 1861), 531 (5th and 6th quotations); Sinha, "Allies for Emancipation?," in Foner, ed., *Our Lincoln*, 177.
15. "Annual Message to Congress," December 3, 1861, *Collected Works*, 5:48–49 (1st–5th quotations); McKivigan, *Forgotten Firebrand*, 70–71; Burlingame, *Lincoln*, 2:236; Smith to Thaddeus Stevens, December 6, 1861, in Harlow, *Smith*, 431–32 (6th and 7th quotations); Garrison to Johnson, December 6, 1861, in Merrill and Ruchames, eds., *Letters of Garrison*, 5:47 (8th and 9th quotations); Stanton to Smith, December 16[, 1861], in Gordon, ed., *Selected Papers of Stanton and Anthony*, 1:470 (10th quotation); Child to John G. Whittier, January 21, 1862, in Holland and Meltzer, eds., *Collected Correspondence of Child* (11th quotation); Child to Mary Stearns, January 30, 1862, in Meltzer and Holland, eds., *Child, Selected Letters*, 399–400, 405 (12th and 13th quotations). See also Sinha, "Allies for Emancipation?," in Foner, ed., *Our Lincoln*, 183–85.
16. Cleveland to Lincoln, January 5, 1861, (1st quotation); Jay to Lincoln, June 29, 1861, Fee to Lincoln, October 3, 1861 (2nd and 3rd quotations), Lincoln Papers; Mayer, *All on Fire*, 521.
17. Conlin, "Abolition Lecture Controversy," 301–23; Conway, *Autobiography*, 1:306–8; Stewart, *Phillips*, 236; *Principia*, April 10, 1862.
18. Conlin, "Abolition Lecture Controversy," 312–14, 317; *Principia*, January 30, 1862 (1st and 2nd quotations); Howard, *Religion*, 24; d'Entremont, *Southern Emancipator*, 161–62; Smith to Webb, March 15, 1862, Garrison Papers (3rd quotation). See also Conway, *Golden Hour*, 11–13.
19. Conway, *Autobiography*, 1:345–47.
20. Howe to F. W. Bird, March 5, 1862, in Richards, ed., *Letters and Journals of Howe*, 500–501 (1st and 2nd quotations); Garrison and Garrison, *Garrison*, 4:47–49; *Liberator*, March 14, 1862; Child to Greeley, March 9, 1862, in Meltzer and Holland, eds., *Child, Selected Letters*, 407; "Lecture by Wendell Phillips, Esq.," *Liberator*, March 14, 1862 (3rd quotation).
21. Stewart, *Phillips*, 231–36; Phillips to Ann Phillips, March 31, 1862, Phillips Papers (1st–3rd quotations); *Principia*, April 10, 1862 (4th and 5th quotations); Burlingame, *Lincoln*, 2:343.
22. Burlingame, *Lincoln*, 2:344–45; Harrison, *Washington*, 114–17; J. McPherson, *Struggle for Equality*, 97–98; Child to Robert Wallcutt, April 20,

1862, Garrison Papers (1st and 2nd quotations); *National Anti-Slavery Standard*, April 26, 1862 (3rd and 4th quotations); *Liberator*, May 16, 23, 1862 (6th quotation; 5th and 6th quotations); Samuel May Jr. (quoting Pillsbury) to Elizabeth Buffum Chace, April 22, 1862, in Wyman and Wyman, *Chace*, 1:236 (7th quotation).

23. Burlingame, *Lincoln*, 2:347; Garrison to Charles B. Sedgewick, May 20, 1862, in Merrill and Ruchames, eds., *Letters of Garrison*, 5:93 (quotations).

24. J. McPherson, *Struggle for Equality*, 106–10; Phillips to Sumner, June 29, 1862, Sumner Papers (1st and 2nd quotations); "Remarks to a Delegation of Progressive Friends," June 20, 1861, *Collected Works*, 5:278–79 (3rd and 4th quotation); Mayer, *All of Fire*, 537–38.

25. "The Slaveholders' Rebellion. A Speech Delivered on the 4th Day of July, 1862," in P. Foner, ed., *Douglass*, 501–2; Burlingame, *Lincoln*, 2:396–98.

26. J. McPherson, *Struggle for Equality*, 111–12; Sanger, ed., *Statutes at Large*, 12:591 (quotation); Burlingame, *Lincoln*, 2:407–10.

27. "Emancipation Proclamation—First Draft," [July 22, 1862], *Collected Works*, 5:336–37 (1st quotation); Gay to Lincoln, July 30, 1862 (2nd quotation); "Enquirer to the Editor of the Tribune," July 28, 1862, Lincoln Papers (3rd quotation).

28. Lincoln to Gay, August 1, 1862, August 8, 1862, Lincoln to Greeley, September 2, 1862, *Collected Works*, 5:353 (1st quotation), 364, 388–89; Starr, *Bohemian Brigade*, 126–27; *New-York Daily Tribune*, August 19, 1862 (2nd quotation).

29. "Address on Colonization to a Deputation of Negroes," August 14, 1862, *Collected Works*, 5:370–72.

30. Purvis to Pomeroy, August 28, 1862, *New-York Daily Tribune*, September 20, 1862 (1st quotation); *Douglass Monthly* 5 (September 1862), 707–8 (2nd quotation); *Liberator*, August 22, 1862 (3rd and 4th quotations); Phillips to Gay, September 2, 1862, Gay Papers (5th quotations).

31. *National Anti-Slavery Standard*, August 30, 1862 (1st–3rd quotations); Gay to Lincoln, August 1862, Lincoln Papers (4th–6th quotations).

32. Garrison to Johnson, September 9, 1862, in Merrill and Ruchames, eds., *Letters of Garrison*, 5:112–13 (1st and 2nd quotations); Phillips to Gay, September 2, 1862, Gay Papers (3rd quotation).

33. "Preliminary Emancipation Proclamation," September 22, 1862, *Collected Works*, 5:433–44 (quotation); Harrold, "Dramatic Turning Point or *Points*?," 15; Sinha, "Architects of Their Own Liberation," 7.

34. Garrison to Fanny Garrison, September 25, 1862, in Merrill and Ruchames, eds., *Letters of Garrison*, 5:114–15 (1st–6th quotations); Hale, ed., *Clarke*, 243; Cheever to Elizabeth, September 29, 1862, Cheever-Wheeler Family Papers; Goodell to Daughter, September 24, 1862, Goodell Family Papers.

35. Donald, *Sumner and the Coming of the Civil War*, 89, 96; Burlingame, *Lincoln*, 2:450; "Annual Message to Congress," December 1, 1862, *Collected Works*, 5:530–35 (1st–3rd quotations); *Commonwealth*, December 6, 1862 (4th quotation); *Liberator*, December 26, 1862 (5th and 6th quotations); Garrison to Johnson, December 26, 1862, in Merrill and Ruchames, eds., *Letters of Garrison*, 5:57 (7th and 8th quotations).
36. Burlingame, *Lincoln*, 2:422; Gienapp, *Lincoln*, 117–18; Child to Sarah Shaw, November 11, 1862, in Meltzer and Holland, eds., *Child, Selected Letters*, 420 (quotation); Cheever to Lincoln, November 22, 1862, Lincoln Papers; Howard, *Religion*, 49–50.
37. J. McPherson, *Struggle for Equality*, 120–21; McFeely, *Douglass*, 215–16; *Liberator*, January 2, 1863 (1st and 2nd quotations); Waterston to Sumner, January 2, 1863, Sumner Papers (3rd quotation).
38. Stewart, *Phillips*, 241–42, 244; *Principia*, January 8, 1863 (1st and 2nd quotations); Tilton to Garrison, January 9, 1863, Garrison/Antislavery Papers (3rd quotation); "Special Meeting of the Executive Committee of the American Anti-Slavery Society," January 13, 1863, *Liberator*, January 16, 1863 (4th quotation); American Anti-Slavery Society, *Proceedings*, 58 (4th quotation).
39. Conway, *Autobiography*, 1:378–81. See also Howard, *Religion*, 57.
40. Stearns, *Life and Public Services of Stearns*, 280 (1st quotation); Conway, *Autobiography*, 340 (2nd and 3rd quotations); "Abraham Lincoln: His Relations to Slavery," *New-York Daily Tribune*, August 30, 1885 (4th quotation).

7. Drawing Closer as Criticism Continues

1. J. McPherson, *Struggle for Equality*, 122–24; Burlingame, *Lincoln*, 2:448, 498–99.
2. Goodell to Lincoln, July 14, 1863, Lincoln Papers.
3. Lincoln to Charles Sumner, June 1, 1863, Lincoln to James Conkling, August 26, 1863, Lincoln to William Birney, October 3, 1863, Lincoln to Maryland Slaveholders, October 21, 1863, *Collected Works*, 6:242–43, 406–10, 495, 529; Gienapp, *Lincoln*, 168–69.
4. Burlingame, *Lincoln*, 2:520–24; Douglass to Stearns, August 12, 1863, in Simpson, Sears, and Sheehan-Dean, eds., *Civil War*, 457–60; American Anti-Slavery Society, *Proceedings*, 116–17 (quotations).
5. American Anti-Slavery Society, *Proceedings*, 117.
6. Lincoln to James Conkling, August 26, 1863, *Collected Works*, 6:407–9 (1st–4th quotations); *Principia*, September 10, 1863 (5th and 6th quotations); Sanborn to Moncure Conway, [November 2, 1863], Conway Papers (7th quotation).
7. Gienapp, *Lincoln*, 140–48.

8. Burlingame, *Lincoln*, 2:543–52, 570, 609–13; Wieck, *Lincoln's Quest*, 47–52; Commager, *Parker*.

9. Samuel Gridley Howe to Frank Bird, September 17, 1862, in Richards, ed., *Letters and Journals of Howe*, 2:502; Wilson, *History of the Antislavery Measures*, 328; J. McPherson, *Struggle for Equality*, 75–79, 188–90; Stanton et al., *History of Woman Suffrage*, 2:26–30; Griffing to Garrison, August 19, 1864, *Liberator*, August 26, 1864; Harrold, *Subversives*, 235–36.

10. E. Foner, *Reconstruction*, 35–37; "Proclamation of Amnesty and Reconstruction," December 8, 1863, *Collected Works*, 7:53–56 (quotations).

11. Phillips to Benjamin Butler, December 13, 1863, in Butler, *Private and Official Correspondence of Butler*, 3:207 (1st and 2nd quotations); *New York Times*, December 23, 1863 (3rd quotation); Wright to Lincoln, December 16, 1863, Lincoln Papers (4th–5th quotations); Lincoln to Wright, December 20, 1863, *Collected Works*, 7:51; J. McPherson, *Struggle for Equality*, 125–26.

12. J. McPherson, *Struggle for Equality*, 260–67; Stewart, *Phillips*, 245–46, 249–50; McDaniel, *Problem of Democracy*, 232–35; Howard, *Religion*, 69–72; Tilton to Wendell Phillips Garrison, December 6, 1863, Garrison Papers (quotations).

13. "Speech of Wendell Phillips, Esq.," January 28[, 1864], "Annual Meeting of the Massachusetts Anti-Slavery Society," January 28, 1864, *Liberator*, February 5, 1864 (quotations); Mayer, *All on Fire*, 562–67; McDaniel, *Problem of Democracy*, 236.

14. *Principia*, March 3, 1864 (1st quotation); Child to Smith, April 22, 1864, Smith Papers (2nd quotation); Garrison to Johnson, April 28, 1864, in Merrill and Ruchames, eds., *Letters of Garrison*, 5:201 (3rd quotation); Cheever to Tilton, [September 1864], Tilton Papers (4th quotation).

15. E. McPherson, *Political History*, 410–14 (quotation); Fremont to Worthington G. Snethen et al., June 4, 1864, *Principia*, June 9, 1864; Johnson to Henry T. Cheever, June 16, 1864, Cheever-Wheeler Family Papers; Howard, *Religion*, 77–78.

16. *Liberator*, March 18, 1864 (quotations); "Thirty-First Anniversary of the American Anti-Slavery Society, May 11, 1864," *Liberator*, May 27, 1864.

17. Garrison to Helen E. Garrison, May 13, 1864, June 8, 1864, in Merrill and Ruchames, eds., *Letters of Garrison*, 5:202–6; *Liberator*, June 24, 1864.

18. Garrison to Helen E. Garrison, June 9, 1864, in Merrill and Ruchames, eds., *Letters of Garrison*, 5:209–10 (1st quotation); Garrison and Garrison, *Garrison*, 4:117 (2nd–4th quotations). See also White, *Visits with Lincoln*, 105–7; Merrill and Ruchames, eds., *Letters of Garrison*, 289–90.

19. J. McPherson, *Struggle for Equality*, 245–46; Donald, *Sumner and the Rights of Man*, 184, 186; Garrison to Francis W. Newman, [July 15, 1864], in Merrill and Ruchames, eds., *Letters of Garrison*, 5:220–23 (quotations); d'Entremont, *Southern Emancipator*, 206–10.

20. Hay entry, May 14, 1864, in Dennett, ed., *Diaries and Letters of John Hay*, 181; Howard, *Religion*, 73; Johnson to Henry T. Cheever, June 16, 1864, Cheever-Wheeler Family Papers (quotation); Garrison and Garrison, *Garrison*, 4:122–24; Stewart, *Phillips*, 253; Howard, *Religion*, 77–78; Cheek and Cheek, *Langston*, 424–25; Pennington to [Robert Hamilton], June 9, 1864, *Weekly Anglo-African*, June 26, 1864; Burlingame, *Lincoln*, 2:640; Smith to Wade and Davis, August 8, 1864, *New-York Daily Tribune*, August 17, 1864 (3rd–5th quotations).

21. Giraud, *Embattled Maiden*, 6–7, 74–78, 80–81 (quotation); Young, "Dickinson and the Civil War," 68–70; Howard, *Religion*, 76–77; Burlingame, *Lincoln*, 2:634–35.

22. Gienapp, *Lincoln*, 167–70; Lincoln to Whom It May Concern, July 18, 1864, Lincoln to Charles D. Robinson, August 16, 1864 (draft), *Collected Works*, 7:451, 499–500; Douglass to Tilton, October 16, 1864, in P. Foner, ed., *Life and Writings of Douglass*, 3:423.

23. Douglass to "an English Correspondent," *Liberator*, September 16, 1864 (1st and 2nd quotations); Douglass to Tilton, October 15, 1864, in P. Foner, ed., *Life and Writings of Douglass*, 3:423 (3rd–10th quotations). See also Eaton, *Grant, Lincoln, and the Freedmen*, 175.

24. Douglass to Tilton, October 15, 1864, P. Foner, ed., *Life and Writings of Douglass*, 3:423–24 (1st–3rd quotations); Eaton, *Grant, Lincoln, and the Freedman*, 175–76 (4th quotation).

25. Douglass to Lincoln, August 29, 1864, Lincoln Papers (1st quotation); J. McPherson, *Struggle for Equality*, 282–85; Donald, *Sumner and the Rights of Man*, 189; Burlingame, *Lincoln*, 2:688–92; Garrison to Samuel J. May, September 6, 1864, in Merrill and Ruchames, eds., *Letters of Garrison*, 5:235; Douglass to Garrison, September 17, 1864, *Liberator*, September 23, 1864 (2nd quotation).

26. Smith to Elizabeth Cady Stanton, October 3, 1864, Stanton Papers (1st quotation); Burlingame, *Lincoln*, 2:634–35; Howard, *Religion*, 86–87; Jeffrey, *Abolitionists Remember*, 226–43; White, *Visits with Lincoln*, 118–23; Truth to Johnson, November 17, 1864, *National Anti-Slavery Standard*, December 17, 1864 (2nd–4th quotations).

27. Stearns to Garrison, September 12, 1864, *Commonwealth*, September 23, 1864 (1st and 2nd quotations); Elizabeth Cady Stanton to Anthony, September 25, 1864, in Stanton and Blatch, eds., *Stanton as Revealed*, 2:100–101 (3rd and 4th quotations); Wilson, *History of the Rise and Fall*, 3:547 (5th and 6th quotations).

28. J. McPherson, *Struggle for Equality*, 285 (1st and 2nd quotation); Phillips to Elizabeth Cady Stanton, November 20, 1864, Stanton Papers (3rd quotation).

29. "Message to Congress," December 6, 1864, in Gienapp, ed., *This Fiery Trial*, 212–15 (1st quotation); Johnson to Lincoln, December 7, 1864, Lincoln Papers (2nd–4th quotations).

30. Stewart, *Phillips*, 254; Elizabeth Cady Stanton to Anthony, December 29, 1864, in Stanton and Blatch, eds., *Stanton as Revealed*, 2:103–4 (quotation).

31. Burlingame, *Lincoln*, 2:749–51; Garnet, *Memorial Discourse*, 69–71; Howard, *Religion*, 168–69.

32. Mayer, *All on Fire*, 576; J. McPherson, *Struggle for Equality*, 294–99; "Freedom Triumphant: Grand Jubilee Meeting . . . ," *Liberator*, March 10, 1865; Garrison to Forbes, January 21, 1865, in Merrill and Ruchames, eds., *Letters of Garrison*, 5:254 (quotation).

33. Garrison to Lincoln, January 21, 1865, in Merrill and Ruchames, eds., *Letters of Garrison*, 5:255–57.

34. Lincoln to Garrison, February 7, 1865, *Liberator*, February 17, 1865; Garrison to Lincoln, February 13, 1865, in Merrill and Ruchames, eds., *Letters of Garrison*, 5:257–58 (quotations).

35. Nicolay and Hay, *Lincoln*, 10:85 (quotation); Pierce, *Sumner*, 4:219; Donald, *Sumner and the Rights of Man*, 204–5.

36. Rice, ed., *Reminiscences of Lincoln*, 191–93 (1st and 2nd quotations).

37. Douglass, *Life and Times of Douglass*, in McKivigan, ed., *Douglass Papers*, series 2, 3:284–85 (3rd–5th quotations); *Liberator*, March 10, 1865 (6th and 7th quotations).

38. J. McPherson, *Struggle for Equality*, 190–91; Chamberlain to Editor, September 22, 1883, *New-York Daily Tribune*, November 4, 1883 (quotations).

39. Garrison to Helen Garrison, April 7, 9, 1865, Garrison to Stanton, September 15, 1865, in Merrill and Ruchames, eds., *Letters of Garrison*, 5:263–70, 295–97; Mayer, *All on Fire*, 577–85.

40. "Abraham Lincoln," in Phillips, *Speeches, Lectures, and Letters*, 2nd series, 447–49.

41. Child to Tilton, May 6, 1865, *Liberator*, May 28, 1865.

42. "Fred. Douglas [*sic*] on President Lincoln . . . ," *New York Times*, June 2, 1865.

43. "Address on the Assassination of Abraham Lincoln," *Liberator*, July 7, 1865.

BIBLIOGRAPHY

This listing includes sections for manuscript collections;
published documents, letters, and papers; newspapers;
and articles, books, and dissertations.

Manuscript Collections

John Quincy Adams Papers, Massachusetts Historical Society, Boston, Mass.

Salmon P. Chase Papers, microfilm edition, John Niven, editor.

Cheever-Wheeler Family Papers, American Antiquarian Society, Worcester, Mass.

Moncure Daniel Conway Papers, Rare Book and Manuscript Library, Columbia University, New York, N.Y.

Wendell Phillips Garrison Papers, Rush Rhees Library, University of Rochester, Rochester, N.Y.

William Lloyd Garrison/Antislavery Papers, Boston Public Library, Boston, Mass.

Sydney Howard Gay Papers, Columbia University, New York, N.Y.

Joshua R. Giddings Papers, Ohio History Connection (formerly Ohio Historical Society), Columbus, Ohio.

William Goodell Family Papers, Berea College, Berea, Ky.

Abraham Lincoln Papers, Library of Congress, Washington, D.C.

Samuel J. May Antislavery Collection, Cornell University Library, Ithaca, N.Y.

Wendell Phillips Papers, Houghton Library, Harvard University, Cambridge, Mass.

William H. Seward Papers, Rush Rhees Library, University of Rochester, Rochester, N.Y.

Gerrit Smith Papers, Syracuse University Library, Syracuse, N.Y.

Elizabeth Cady Stanton Papers, Library of Congress, Washington, D.C.

Boyd B. Stutler Collection, West Virginia State Archives, Charleston, W.Va.

Charles Sumner Papers, Houghton Library, Harvard University, Cambridge, Mass.

Eli Thayer Papers, Brown University Library, Providence, R.I.

Theodore Tilton Papers, New-York Historical Society, Albany, N.Y.

Published Documents, Letters, and Papers

Alvord, Clarence Walworth, ed. *Governor Edward Coles*. Springfield: Illinois State Historical Library, 1920.

American and Foreign Anti-Slavery Society. *[Eighth] Annual Report . . . May 9, 1848.* New York: American and Foreign Anti-Slavery Society, 1848.

American Anti-Slavery Society. *Proceedings of the American Anti-Slavery Society, at Its Third Decade . . . Dec. 3d and 4th, 186[3].* New York: American Anti-Slavery Society, 1864.

American Convention. *Minutes of the Proceedings of a Special Meeting of the Fifteenth American Convention for Promoting the Abolition of Slavery . . . .* Philadelphia: American Convention, 1818.

Blassingame, John W., et al., eds. *The Frederick Douglass Papers.* Series 1, *Speeches, Debates, and Interviews.* 4 vols. New Haven, Conn.: Yale University Press, 1979–92.

Bowen, A. L. "Anti-Slavery Convention Held in Alton, Illinois, October 26–28, 1837." *Journal of the Illinois State Historical Society* 20 (October 1927): 329–56.

Butler, Benjamin F. *Private and Official Correspondence of Gen. Benjamin F. Butler during the period of the Civil War.* 5 vols. Norwood, Mass.: Plimpton Press, 1917.

Child, Lydia Maria. *Letters of Lydia Maria Child.* Boston: Houghton, Mifflin, 1883.

Clarke, James Freeman. *James Freeman Clarke: Autobiography, Diary, and Correspondence.* Edited by Edward Everett Hale. Boston: Houghton, Mifflin, 1891.

Commager, Henry Steele, ed. *Theodore Parker: An Anthology.* Boston: Beacon Press, 1960.

Congressional Globe. Washington, D.C.: Blair and Rives, 1834–73.

Conway, Moncure Daniel. *Autobiography, Memories, and Experiences of Moncure Daniel Conway.* 2 vols. New York: Cassell, 1904.

———. *The Golden Hour.* Boston: Ticknor and Fields, 1862.

Copeland, David A., ed. *The Antebellum Era: Primary Documents on Events from 1820 to 1860.* Westport, Conn.: Greenwood Press, 2003.

Dennett, Tyler, ed. *Lincoln and the Civil War in the Diaries and Letters of John Hay.* New York: Dodd, Mead, 1939.

Douglass, Frederick. "Oration in Memory of Abraham Lincoln, Delivered at the Unveiling of the Freedmen's Monument in Memory of Abraham Lincoln, in Lincoln Park, Washington, D.C., April 14, 1876." River Campus Libraries, University of Rochester, Frederick Douglass Project. N.d. Accessed August 27, 2016. http://rbscp.lib.rochester.edu/4402.

Duberman, Martin B., ed. *The Antislavery Vanguard: New Essays on the Abolitionists.* Princeton, N.J.: Princeton University Press, 1965.

Dublin, Michael J., ed. *United States Congressional Elections, 1788–1997: The Official Results.* Jefferson, N.C.: McFarland, 1998.

Eaton, John. *Grant, Lincoln, and the Freedmen: Reminiscences of the Civil War*. New York: Longmans, Green, 1907.

Fehrenbacher, Don E., ed. *Lincoln: Speeches and Writings, 1859–1865*. 2 vols. New York: Library of America, 1989.

Flint, Henry Martyn. *Life of Stephen A. Douglas, to Which Are Added His Speeches and Reports*. Philadelphia: John E. Potter, 1863.

Foner, Philip S., ed. *Frederick Douglass: Selected Speeches and Writings*. Abridged and adapted by Yuval Taylor. Chicago: Lawrence Hill Books, 1999.

———. *The Life and Writings of Frederick Douglass*. 5 vols. New York: International Publishers, 1950–75.

Garrison, William Lloyd, ed. *The Abolition of Slavery: The Rights of the Government under the War Power*. Boston: B. F. Wallcut, 1862.

Garnet, Henry Highland. *A Memorial Discourse Delivered in the House of Representatives, Washington, D.C. on Sabbath, February 12, 1865*. Philadelphia: Joseph M. Wilson, 1865.

Gates, Henry, Louis, Jr., ed. *Douglass Autobiographies: Narrative of the Life, My Bondage and My Freedom, Life and Times*. New York: Library of America, 1994.

Giddings, Joshua R. *Speeches in Congress*. 1853. Reprint, New York: Negro Universities Press, 1968.

Gienapp, William E., ed. *This Fiery Trial: The Speeches and Writings of Abraham Lincoln*. New York: Oxford University Press, 2002.

Goodell, William, and Gerrit Smith. *Address of the Macedon Convention by William Goodell and Letters of Gerrit Smith*. Albany, N.Y.: S. W. Green, 1847.

Gordon, Ann D., ed. *The Selected Papers of Elizabeth Cady Stanton and Susan B. Anthony*. 4 vols. New Brunswick, N.J.: Rutgers University Press, 1997.

Hertz, Emanuel, ed. *The Hidden Lincoln: From the Letters and Papers of William H. Herndon*. New York: Blue Ribbon Books, 1940.

Holland, Patricia G., and Milton Meltzer, eds. *The Collected Correspondence of Lydia Maria Child, 1817–1880*. Millwood, N.Y.: Kraus Microform, 1979.

Johannsen, Robert W., ed. *The Lincoln-Douglas Debates of 1858*. New York: Oxford University Press, 1965.

Journal of the House of Representatives, 30th Cong., 2nd Sess. (December 21, 1848).

Lincoln, Abraham. *The Collected Works of Abraham Lincoln*. Edited by Roy P. Basler. 9 vols. New Brunswick, N.J.: Rutgers University Press, 1953–55.

Linden, Glenn M., comp. *Voices from the Gathering Storm: The Coming of the American Civil War*. Wilmington, Del.: Scholarly Resources, 2001.

Lowance, Mason I., Jr., ed. *A House Divided: The Antebellum Slavery Debates in America, 1776–1865*. Princeton, N.J.: Princeton University Press, 2003.

Mallory, Daniel, ed. *The Life and Speeches of the Hon. Henry Clay*. 2 vols. New York: Robert P. Bixby, 1843.

Massachusetts Anti-Slavery Society. *Twenty-First Annual Report . . . January 26, 1853*. Boston: Massachusetts Anti-Slavery Society, 1853.

Meltzer, Milton, and Patricia G. Holland, eds. *Lydia Maria Child, Selected Letters, 1817–1880*. Amherst: University of Massachusetts Press, 1982.

Merrill, Walter M., and Louis Ruchames, eds. *The Letters of William Lloyd Garrison*. 6 vols. Cambridge, Mass.: Harvard University Press, 1971–81.

Moses, William Jeremiah, ed., *Classical Black Nationalism: From the American Revolution to Marcus Garvey*. New York: New York University Press, 1961.

Niven, John, et al., eds. *The Salmon P. Chase Papers*. 5 vols. Kent, Ohio: Kent State University Press, 1993–98.

Ohio Anti-Slavery Society. *Report of the Second Anniversary . . . Twenty-Seventh of April, 1837*. Cincinnati: Ohio Anti-Slavery Society, 1837.

Palmer, Beverly Wilson. *The Selected Letters of Charles Sumner*. 2 vols. Boston: Northeastern University Press, 1990.

Parker, Theodore. *The Present Aspect of Slavery in America and the Immediate Duty of the North . . . January 29, 1858*. Boston: Bela Marsh, 1858.

———. *A Sermon of the Dangers Which Threaten the Rights of Man in America . . . July 2, 1854*. Boston: Benjamin B. Mussey, 1854.

Pierce, Edward L. *Memoir and Letters of Charles Sumner*. 4 vols. 1877–93. Reprint, New York: Arno Press, 1969.

Phillips, Wendell. *Speeches, Lectures, and Letters*. Boston: Lee and Shepard, 1884.

———. *Speeches, Lectures, and Letters*. 2nd series. Boston: Lee and Shepard, 1905.

Pickard, John B., ed. *The Letters of John Greenleaf Whittier*. 3 vols. Cambridge, Mass.: Harvard University Press, 1975.

Pickard, Samuel T. *Life and Letters of John Greenleaf Whittier*. 2 vols. Boston: Houghton, Mifflin, 1894.

Rice, Allen Thorndike, ed. *Reminiscences of Abraham Lincoln by Distinguished Men of His Time*. 1886. Reprint, New York: Haskell House, 1971.

Richards, Laura E., ed. *Letters and Journals of Samuel Gridley Howe*. Boston: Dana Estes, 1909.

Ripley, C. Peter, et al., eds. *The Black Abolitionist Papers*. 5 vols. Chapel Hill: University of North Carolina Press, 1985–92.

Sanger, George P., ed. *The Statutes at Large, Treaties, and Proclamations of the United States of America . . . .* 18 vols. Boston: Little, Brown, 1863–69.

Scarborough, William Kauffman, ed. *The Diary of Edmund Ruffin*. 3 vols. Baton Rouge: Louisiana State University Press, 1972.

Simpson, Brooks D., Stephen W. Sears, and Aaron Sheehan-Dean, eds. *The Civil War: The Third Year . . . Told by Those Who Lived It*. New York: Library of America, 2013.

Smith, Gerrit. *Gerrit Smith to Owen Lovejoy, July 12, 1861*. Peterboro, N.Y.: privately published, 1861.

———. *Speeches of Gerrit Smith in Congress*. New York: Mason Brothers, 1855.

Sparks, Edwin Erle, ed. *Collections of the Illinois State Historical Library*. Vol. 3, *Lincoln Series, Vol. 1: The Lincoln-Douglas Debates of 1858*. Springfield: Illinois State Historical Library, 1908.

Stanton, Theodore, and Harriet Stanton Blatch, eds. *Elizabeth Cady Stanton as Revealed in Her Letters, Diary, and Reminiscences*. 2 vols. New York: Harper and Brothers, 1922.

Weiss, John. *Life and Correspondence of Theodore Parker, Minister of the Twenty-Eighth Congregational Society, Boston*. 2 vols. New York: D. Appleton, 1864.

Willard, Samuel. "Personal Reminiscences of Life in Illinois—1830 to 1850." *Transactions of the Illinois State Historical Society* 11 (1906): 73–87.

Wilson, Douglas L., and Rodney O. Davis, eds. *Herndon's Informants: Letters, Interviews, and Statements about Abraham Lincoln*. Urbana: University of Illinois Press, 1997.

Woolley, John, and Gerhard Peters. *The American Presidency Project*. 1999–2017. Accessed April 5, 2016. http://www.presidency.ucsb.edu.

Wright, Elizur. *An Eye Opener for the Wide Awakes*. Boston: Thayer and Eldridge, 1860.

Newspapers

Anti-Slavery Bugle (Salem, Ohio)
Charleston (S.C.) Mercury
Commonwealth (Boston)
Daily Illinois State Register (Springfield)
Douglass Monthly (Rochester, N.Y.)
Frederick Douglass' Paper (Rochester, N.Y.)
Free West (Chicago)
Illinois Daily State Journal (Springfield)
Liberator (Boston)
National Anti-Slavery Standard (New York)
National Era (Washington, D.C.)
New-York Daily Tribune
New York Herald
New York Times
North Star (Rochester, N.Y.)
Principia (New York)
Weekly Anglo-African (New York)

Articles, Books, and Dissertations

Abbott, Richard H. *Cobbler in Congress: The Life of Henry Wilson, 1812–1875.* Lexington: University Press of Kentucky, 1972.

Baer, Helene Gilbert. *The Heart Is Like Heaven: The Life of Lydia Maria Child.* Philadelphia: University of Pennsylvania Press, 1964.

Bemis, Samuel Flagg. *John Quincy Adams and the Union.* New York: Alfred A. Knopf, 1956.

Berwanger, Eugene H. *The Frontier against Slavery: Western Anti-Negro Prejudice and the Slavery Extension Controversy.* Urbana: University of Illinois Press, 1967.

Blanchard, Rufus. *Discovery and Conquests of the Northwest, with the History of Chicago.* Wheaton, Ill.: R. Blanchard, 1879.

Blue, Frederick J. *The Free Soilers: Third Party Politics, 1848–1854.* Urbana: University of Illinois Press, 1973.

———. *Salmon P. Chase: A Life in Politics.* Kent, Ohio: Kent State University Press, 1987.

Browne, Francis F. *The Everyday Life of Abraham Lincoln.* Lincoln: University of Nebraska Press, 1995.

Browne, Robert H. *Abraham Lincoln and the Men of His Time.* 2 vols. Cincinnati, Ohio: Jennings and Pye, 1901.

Burin, Eric. *Slavery and the Peculiar Solution: A History of the American Colonization Society.* Gainesville: University Press of Florida, 2006.

Burlingame, Michael. *Abraham Lincoln: A Life.* 2 vols. Baltimore: Johns Hopkins University Press, 2008.

———. *The Inner World of Abraham Lincoln.* Urbana: University of Illinois Press, 1994.

Campanella, Richard. *Lincoln in New Orleans: The 1828–1831 Flatboat Voyages and Their Place in History.* Lafayette: University of Louisiana at Lafayette Press, 2010.

Cheek, William, and Aimee Lee Cheek. *John Mercer Langston and the Fight for Black Freedom, 1829–65.* Urbana: University of Illinois Press, 1989.

Codding, Hannah P. "Biographical Sketch of Ichabod Codding." *Proceedings of the State Historical Society of Wisconsin at the Forty-Fifth Annual Meeting Held December 9 and 16, 1897.* Madison: Democratic Printing, 1898. 171–96.

Commager, Henry Steele. *Theodore Parker.* Boston: Beacon Press, 1947.

Conlin, Michael F. "The Smithsonian Abolition Lecture Controversy: The Clash of Antislavery Politics with American Science in Wartime Washington." *Civil War History* 46 (December 2000): 301–23.

Cooper, William J., Jr. *The South and the Politics of Slavery, 1828–1856.* Baton Rouge: Louisiana State University Press, 1978.

d'Entremont, John. *Southern Emancipator: Moncure Conway—the American Years, 1832–1865*. New York: Oxford University Press, 1987.

Dillon, Merton L. *The Abolitionists: The Growth of a Dissenting Minority*. New York: W. W. Norton, 1979.

———. *Benjamin Lundy and the Struggle for Negro Freedom*. Urbana: University of Illinois Press, 1966.

———. *Elijah P. Lovejoy, Abolitionist Editor*. Urbana: University of Illinois Press, 1961.

Donald, David Herbert. *Charles Sumner and the Coming of the Civil War*. Chicago: Chicago University Press, 1960.

———. *Charles Sumner and the Rights of Man*. New York: Alfred A. Knopf, 1970.

———. *Lincoln's Herndon*. New York: Alfred A. Knopf, 1948.

Douglass, Frederick. *Life and Times of Frederick Douglass*. In *The Frederick Douglass Papers*, series 2, *Autobiographical Writings*, vol. 3, edited by John R. McKivigan. New Haven, Conn.: Yale University Press, 2012.

Egerton, Douglas R. *Year of Meteors: Stephen Douglas, Abraham Lincoln, and the Election That Brought on the Civil War*. New York: Bloomsbury Press, 2010.

Fehrenbacher, Don E. *The Dred Scott Case: Its Significance in American Law and Politics*. New York: Oxford University Press, 1978.

Filler, Louis. *The Crusade against Slavery, 1830–1860*. New York: Harper and Brothers, 1960.

Foner, Eric. *The Fiery Trial: Abraham Lincoln and American Slavery*. New York: W. W. Norton, 2010.

———. *Reconstruction: America's Unfinished Revolution, 1863–1877*. New York: Oxford University Press, 1988.

Forbes, Robert Pierce. *The Missouri Compromise and Its Aftermath: Slavery and the Meaning of America*. Chapel Hill: University of North Carolina Press, 2007.

Freehling, William W. *The Road to Disunion*. 2 vols. New York: Oxford University Press, 1990, 2007.

Friedman, Lawrence J. *Gregarious Saints: Self and Community in American Abolitionism, 1830–1870*. New York: Cambridge University Press, 1982.

Frothingham, Octavius Brooks. *Theodore Parker: A Biography*. New York: G. P. Putnam's Sons, 1880.

Garrison, Wendell Phillips, and Francis Jackson Garrison. *William Lloyd Garrison, 1805–1879: The Story of His Life Told by His Children*. 4 vols. New York: Century, 1885–89.

Gienapp, William E. *Abraham Lincoln and Civil War America: A Biography*. New York: Oxford University Press, 2001.

———. *The Origins of the Republican Party, 1852–1856*. New York: Oxford University Press, 1987.

Giraud, Chester. *Embattled Maiden: The Life of Anna Dickinson*. New York: G. P. Putnam's Sons, 1951.

Glickstein, Jonathan A. "The Chattelization of Northern Whites: An Evolving Abolitionist Warning." *American Nineteenth Century History* 4 (March 2003): 25–58.

Goodheart, Lawrence B. *Abolitionist, Actuary, Atheist: Elizur Wright and the Reform Impulse*. Kent, Ohio: Kent State University Press, 1990.

Guelzo, Allen C. *Abraham Lincoln: Redeemer President*. Grand Rapids, Mich.: William B. Eerdmans, 1999.

Hagedorn, Ann. *Beyond the River: The Untold Story of the Heroes of the Underground Railroad*. New York: Simon and Schuster, 2002.

Hale, Edward E., ed. *James Freeman Clarke*. Boston: Houghton, Mifflin, 1891.

Hamilton, Holman. *Prologue to Conflict: The Crisis and Compromise of 1850*. Lexington: University Press of Kentucky, 1964.

Harlow, Ralph Volney. *Gerrit Smith, Philanthropist and Reformer*. New York: Henry Holt, 1938.

Harrison, Robert. *Washington during Civil War and Reconstruction: Race and Radicalism*. New York: Cambridge University Press, 2011.

Harrold, Stanley. *The Abolitionists and the South, 1831–1861*. Lexington: University Press of Kentucky, 1995.

———. *Border War: Fighting over Slavery before the Civil War*. Chapel Hill: University of North Carolina Press, 2010.

———. "Dramatic Turning Point or *Points*? Teaching Lincoln's Emancipation Proclamation." *OAH Magazine of History* 27 (April 2013): 11–16.

———. *Gamaliel Bailey and Antislavery Union*. Kent, Ohio: Kent State University Press, 1986.

———. *The Rise of Aggressive Abolitionism: Addresses to the Slaves*. Lexington: University Press of Kentucky, 2004.

———. *Subversives: Antislavery Community in Washington, D.C., 1828–1865*. Baton Rouge: Louisiana State University Press, 2003.

Hart, Richard E. "The Underground Railroad." *Lincoln's Springfield*. January 24, 2007. Accessed May 16, 2015. http://lincolnsspringfield.blogspot.com/search/label/The%20Underground%20Railroad.

Herndon, William H., and Jesse W. Weik. *Herndon's Lincoln: The True Story of a Great Life*. 3 vols. Chicago: Belford, Clark, 1889.

Holt, Michael F. *The Rise and Fall of the American Whig Party: Jacksonian Politics and the Onset of the Civil War*. New York: Oxford University Press, 1993.

Horton, James Oliver, and Lois E. Horton. *In Hope of Liberty: Culture, Community, and Protest among Northern Free Blacks, 1700–1860*. New York: Oxford University Press, 1997.

Howard, Victor B. *Religion and the Radical Republican Movement, 1860–1870.* Lexington: University Press of Kentucky, 1990.

Howe, Daniel Walker. *The Political Culture of the American Whigs.* Chicago: University of Chicago Press, 1979.

Huggins, Benjamin L. *Willie Mangum and the North Carolina Whigs in the Age of Jackson.* Jefferson, N.C.: McFarland, 2016.

Huston, James L. "The Experiential Basis of the Northern Antislavery Impulse." *Journal of Southern History* 56 (November 1990): 609–40.

Jeffrey, Julie Roy. *Abolitionists Remember: Antislavery Autobiographies and the Unfinished Work of Emancipation.* Chapel Hill: University of North Carolina Press, 2008

Johannsen, Robert W. *Stephen A. Douglas.* Urbana: University of Illinois Press, 1973.

Johnson, Clifton H. "The American Missionary Association: A Study of Christian Abolitionism." PhD diss., University of North Carolina, 1958.

Johnson, Reinhard O. *The Liberty Party, 1840–1848: Antislavery Third-Party Politics in the United States.* Baton Rouge: Louisiana State University Press, 2009.

Julian, George W. *The Life of Joshua R. Giddings.* Chicago: A. C. McClurg, 1892.

Kaplan, Fred. *Lincoln and the Abolitionists: John Quincy Adams, Slavery, and the Civil War.* New York: HarperCollins, 2017.

Locke, Mary Stoughton. *Anti-Slavery in America, from the Introduction of African Slaves to the Prohibition of the Slave Trade, 1619–1808.* 1901. Reprint, Gloucester, Mass.: Peter Smith, 1965.

Logan, Doug. "William S. Bailey: Abolitionist Editor in the Slave State of Kentucky." NEH Landmarks of American History, Kentucky Historical Society. August 8, 2013. Accessed September 1, 2015. http://history .ky.gov/landmark/william-s-bailey-abolitionist-editor-in-the-slave-state -of-kentucky/.

Magdol, Edward. *Owen Lovejoy: Abolitionist in Congress.* New Brunswick, N.J.: Rutgers University Press, 1967.

Mayer, Henry. *All on Fire: William Lloyd Garrison and the Abolition of Slavery.* New York: St. Martin's Press, 1998.

Mayfield, John. *Rehearsal for Republicanism: Free Soil and the Politics of Antislavery.* Washington, N.Y.: Kennikat Press, 1980.

McDaniel, W. Caleb. *The Problem of Democracy in the Age of Slavery: Garrisonian Abolitionists and Transatlantic Reform.* Baton Rouge: Louisiana State University Press, 2013.

McFeely, William S. *Frederick Douglass.* New York: Simon and Schuster, 1991.

McKivigan, John R. *Forgotten Firebrand: James Redpath and the Making of Nineteenth-Century America*. Ithaca, N.Y.: Cornell University Press, 2008.

———. *The War against Proslavery Religion: Abolitionism and the Northern Churches, 1830–1865*. Ithaca, N.Y.: Cornell University Press, 1984.

McPherson, Edward. *The Political History of the United States of America, during the Great Rebellion . . . .* Washington, D.C.: Philp and Solomons, 1864.

McPherson, James M. *The Struggle for Equality: Abolitionists and the Negro in the Civil War and Reconstruction*. 2nd ed. Princeton, N.J.: Princeton University Press, 1995.

Mintz, Steven. *Moralists and Modernizers: America's Pre–Civil War Reformers*. Baltimore: Johns Hopkins University Press, 1996.

Moore, Glover. *The Missouri Controversy, 1819–1821*. Lexington: University of Kentucky Press, 1953.

Nash, Gary B. *Race and Revolution*. Madison, Wisc.: Madison House, 1990.

Nevins, Allan. *Ordeal of the Union*. 2 vols. New York: Charles Scribner's Sons, 1947.

Newman, Richard S. *The Transformation of American Abolitionism: Fighting Slavery in the Early Republic*. Chapel Hill: University of North Carolina Press, 2002.

Newton, John Fort. *Lincoln and Herndon*. Cedar Rapids, Iowa: Torch Press, 1910.

Nicolay, John G., and John Hay. *Abraham Lincoln: A History*. 10 vols. New York: Century, 1917.

Norman, Matthew. "The Other Lincoln-Douglas Debate: The Race Issue in a Comparative Context." *Journal of the Abraham Lincoln Association* 31 (Winter 2010): 1–21.

Oates, Stephen B. *Abraham Lincoln: The Man behind the Myths*. New York: Harper and Row, 1984.

———. *To Purge This Land with Blood: A Biography of John Brown*. 2nd ed. Amherst: University of Massachusetts Press, 1984.

Pasternak, Martin B. *Rise Now and Fly to Arms: The Life of Henry Highland Garnet*. New York: Garland, 1995.

Pease, Jane H., and William H. Pease. *They Who Would Be Free: Blacks' Search for Freedom, 1830–1861*. New York: Atheneum, 1974.

Perry, Lewis. *Radical Abolitionism: Anarchy and the Government of God in Antislavery Thought*. Ithaca, N.Y.: Cornell University Press, 1973.

Potter, David M. *The Impending Crisis, 1848–1861*. New York: Harper and Row, 1976.

Price, Robert. "The Ohio Anti-Slavery Convention of 1836." *Ohio State Archaeological and Historical Quarterly* 45 (April 1936): 173–88.

Quarles, Benjamin. *Black Abolitionists*. 1969. Reprint, New York: Oxford University Press, 1977.

Remini, Robert V. *Andrew Jackson*. New York: Harper and Row, 1969.

———. *Henry Clay: Statesman for the Union*. New York: W. W. Norton, 1991.

Reynolds, David S. *John Brown, Abolitionist: The Man Who Killed Slavery, Sparked the Civil War, and Seeded Civil Rights*. New York: Alfred A. Knopf, 2005.

Robertson, Stacey M. *Parker Pillsbury: Radical Abolitionist, Male Feminist*. Ithaca, N.Y.: Cornell University Press, 2000.

Russo, Peggy A., and Paul Finkelman, eds. *Terrible Swift Sword: The Legacy of John Brown*. Athens: Ohio University Press, 2005.

Schroeder, John H. *Mr. Polk's War: American Opposition and Dissent, 1846–1848*. Madison: University of Wisconsin Press, 1973.

Scott, Otto. *The Secret Six: John Brown and the Abolitionist Movement*. New York: New York Times Books, 1979.

Sewell, Richard H. *Ballots for Freedom: Antislavery Politics in the United States, 1837–1860*. New York: Oxford University Press, 1976.

Sinha, Manisha. "Allies for Emancipation? Lincoln and Black Abolitionists." In *Our Lincoln: New Perspectives on Lincoln and His World*, edited by Eric Foner, 167–96. New York: W. W. Norton, 2008.

———. "Architects of Their Own Liberation: African Americans, Emancipation, and the Civil War." *OAH Magazine of History* 27 (April 2013): 5–10.

———. *The Slave's Cause: A History of Abolition*. New Haven, Conn.: Yale University Press, 2016.

Stanton, Elizabeth Cady, Susan B. Anthony, Matilda Joslyn Gage, and Ida Husted Harper. *History of Woman Suffrage*. 6 vols. New York: Fowler and Wells, 1881–1922.

Starr, Louis Morris. *Bohemian Brigade: Civil War Newsmen in Action*. New York: Alfred A. Knopf, 1954.

Staudenraus, P. J. *The African Colonization Movement, 1816–1865*. New York: Columbia University Press, 1961.

Stearns, Frank Preston. *The Life and Public Services of George Luther Stearns*. Philadelphia: J. B. Lippincott, 1907.

Stevens, Walter B. *A Reporter's Lincoln*. Edited by Michael Burlingame. 1916. Reprint, Lincoln: University of Nebraska Press, 1998.

Stewart, James Brewer. *Holy Warriors: The Abolitionists and American Slavery*. Rev. ed. New York: Hill and Wang, 1997.

———. *Joshua R. Giddings and the Tactics of Radical Politics*. Cleveland, Ohio: Case Western Reserve University Press, 1970.

———. "Peaceful Hopes and Violent Experiences: The Evolution of Reforming and Radical Abolitionism, 1831–1837." *Civil War History* 17 (December 1971): 293–309.

———. *Wendell Phillips: Liberty's Hero*. Baton Rouge: Louisiana State University Press, 1986.

———. *William Lloyd Garrison and the Challenge of Emancipation.* Arlington Heights, Ill.: Harlan Davidson, 1992.

Thomas, John L. *The Liberator: William Lloyd Garrison—a Biography.* Boston: Little, Brown, 1963.

Trefousse, Hans L. *The Radical Republicans: Lincoln's Vanguard for Racial Justice.* New York: Alfred A. Knopf, 1969.

Volpe, Vernon L. *Forlorn Hope of Freedom: The Liberty Party in the Old Northwest, 1838–1848.* Kent, Ohio: Kent State University Press, 1990.

Walters, Ronald G. *American Reformers, 1815–1860.* New York: Hill and Wang, 1978.

Washburne, Elihu B. *Sketch of Edward Coles, Second Governor of Illinois, and of the Slavery Struggle of 1823–4.* Chicago: Jansen, McClurg, 1882.

Weik, Jesse W. *The Real Lincoln: A Portrait.* Boston: Houghton, Mifflin, 1922.

White, Barbara A. *Visits with Lincoln: Abolitionists Meet the President at the White House.* Lanham, Md.: Lexington Books, 2011.

Whitney, Henry C. *Lincoln the Citizen (February 12, 1809, to March 4, 1861).* New York: Current Literature, 1907.

Wiecek, William M. *The Sources of Antislavery Constitutionalism in America, 1760–1848.* Ithaca, N.Y.: Cornell University Press, 1977.

Wieck, Carl F. *Lincoln's Quest of Equality: The Road to Gettysburg.* DeKalb: Northern Illinois University Press, 2002.

Wilson, Henry. *History of the Antislavery Measures of the Thirty-Seventh and Thirty-Eighth United-States Congresses, 1861–65.* 2nd ed. Boston: Walker, Fuller, 1865.

———. *History of the Rise and Fall of the Slave Power in America.* 3 vols. Boston: J. R. Osgood, 1872–77.

Wiltse, Charles M. *The New Nation, 1800–1845.* New York: Hill and Wang, 1961.

Wright, Philip Green, and Elizabeth Q. Wright. *Elizur Wright: The Father of Life Insurance.* Chicago: University of Chicago Press, 1937.

Wyatt-Brown, Bertram. "The Abolitionists' Postal Campaign of 1835." *Journal of Negro History* 50 (October 1965): 227–38.

———. *Lewis Tappan and the Evangelical War against Slavery.* Baton Rouge: Louisiana State University Press, 1969.

Wyman, Lillie Buffam Chace, and Arthur Crawford Wyman. *Elizabeth Buffum Chace, 1806–1899: Her Life and Its Environment.* 2 vols. Boston: W. B. Clarke, 1914.

Yannessa, Mary Ann. *Levi Coffin, Quaker: Breaking the Bonds of Slavery in Ohio and Indiana.* Richmond, Ind.: Friends United Press, 2001.

Young, James Harvey. "Anna Elizabeth Dickinson and the Civil War: For and against Lincoln." *Mississippi Valley Historical Review* 31 (June 1944): 59–80.

INDEX

abolitionists: and black rights, 54–55, 105, 107; and Civil War, 78–79, 80, 83; and colonization, 10–11; compared to Lincoln, 25–29, 36, 38, 66, 76–77; and Compromise of 1850, 30; on District of Columbia, 85; divide on Lincoln, 94–95, 96–97, 103, 106; on Emancipation Proclamation, 90–92, 95; and Frémont, 107; and fugitive slaves, 31; goals of, 1–2; and Illinois, 7–8, 13, 20–21; and Lincoln, 4, 7, 13, 17, 19–21, 25, 27, 39, 53, 55–56, 59–60, 63, 67–68, 75–76, 82–84, 86, 92–93; on Lincoln, 1–2, 49, 70–74, 77–78, 80, 84–87, 90–91, 97–98, 105, 109–11; Lincoln on, 2, 5, 14–16, 31, 39, 76, 108–9; opposition to, 14, 18; popularity of, 79; and Republicans, 49–50, 52, 67, 69, 86; on slavery expansion, 17, 21–22, 51, 54; and violent means, 52–64; and Whigs, 13
abolitionists, black, 11
abolitionists, church-oriented, 72–73
abolitionists, evangelical, 18
abolitionists, Garrisonian, 18; disagreements among, 67; and disunionism, 51, 78; on Kansas-Nebraska Act, 33–34; on Lincoln, 70–71; on Mexican War, 22; and slave rebellion, 64
abolitionists, immediate, 12–13
abolitionists, moderate Liberty, 19, 26
abolitionists, Quaker, 4–5, 7, 12, 78
abolitionists, radical political: on Civil War, 79; increasing militancy of, 67; on Kansas-Nebraska Act, 33–34; on Lincoln, 70–71, 76; views of, 19, 33–34
abolition movement, 4–5, 10–12, 17–18, 30–31
Adams, John Quincy, 6, 9, 21–22, 79
African Americans: and abolitionists, 1, 10–12; and colonization, 10–11; kidnapping of, 7–8; and Lincoln, 6, 8, 88, 103–4; Lincoln on, 32, 35–36, 51, 53–54, 63, 76, 88, 103–4; rights of, 4; and slavery, 5; and Union armies, 81
American Anti-Slavery Society, 12–13, 15, 92, 101
American Colonization Society, 10–12, 31–33
American Convention for Promoting the Abolition of Slavery, 5, 7
American Indians, 9, 11
American Missionary Association, 18, 67
American Party, 36. *See also* Know-Nothings
Andrew, John A., 67
Anthony, Susan B., 100
Atchison, David, 37

Bailey, Gamaliel, 19, 23–25
Bailey, William S., 60, 72
Banks, Nathaniel P., 55
Bassett, George W., 80
Bates, Edward, 62
Battle of Bull Run, 80
Beecher, Edward, 15
Bell, John, 68
Birney, James G., 11, 19–20, 32